In the Waiting

DRAWING NEAR TO GOD IN SEASONS OF WANTING

JAZMIN N. FRANK

© 2020 Jazmin N. Frank

Printed in the United States of America

All rights reserved. No portion of this book may be reproduced, stored in a retrieval system, or transmitted in any form or by any means—electronic, mechanical, photocopy, recording, scanning, or other—without the prior written permission of the publisher. The only exception is brief quotations in printed reviews and certain other noncommercial uses permitted by copyright law.

www.jazminnfrank.com

Cover & interior design by Typewriter Creative Co. Cover illustrations by wulano and ArtCreationsDesign on CreativeMarket.com.

Scripture quotations marked CSB have been taken from the Christian Standard Bible®, Copyright © 2017 by Holman Bible Publishers. Used by permission. Christian Standard Bible® and CSB® are federally registered trademarks of Holman Bible Publishers.

ISBN 978-0-578-75533-5 (Paperback)
ISBN 978-0-578-75736-0 (eBook)

As a women's ministry leader, I struggle to find devotionals that are grounded in Scripture and pose insightful questions encouraging spiritual growth. Thankfully, *In the Waiting: Drawing Near to God in Seasons of Wanting*, does both! If you feel stuck in a season of waiting, join Jazmin on a journey through God's Word, where you'll discover how to refocus your heart and meet God in the waiting.

— CYNDEE OWNBEY, Author of *Rethinking Women's Ministry* and founder of Women's Ministry Toolbox

I have enjoyed Jazmin's writing for many years and this devotional reflects her faithful study and diligent application of God's Word. We all struggle with seasons of waiting, yet the Bible is filled with stories of God at work in the waiting. I am confident that you will be encouraged by this study of biblical characters, who were ministered to by God, as they learned to trust Him even when the blessing, or promise, was delayed. Forty days from now, you will have a fresh perspective and renewed hope that our God can use seasons of waiting in our life and circumstance for His glory.

— SARAH KOONTZ, Bible Study Author and founder of Living by Designs Ministries

Jazmin Frank does more than simply bridge the head and the heart in this bold daily devotional. She empowers the reader to become a more whole person, which God created them to be. She doesn't pull any punches and she doesn't leave you feeling alone. This specific topic of waiting is one of the biggest spiritual needs in America today.

— JACOB JUNKER, friend

Do you feel stuck and frustrated in your season of waiting? Jazmin Frank offers hope in the waiting. Through brief devotions that touch on many Bible stories, you'll find affirmation and practical tips to help you wait with greater faith.

— SARAH GERINGER, speaker, blogger and author of *Transforming Your Thought Life: Christian Meditation in Focus*

Most of us are familiar with the struggle of wanting something to happen while waiting for God's plan to unfold. This gap between what is and what will be is the focus of *In the Waiting*. In this study, Jazmin explores how we can be active in the present as we hope for the future by examining the stories of beloved Biblical characters. Through their lives we are reminded of God's providence and challenged to trust Him no matter the timetable or answer He gives. Thank you Jazmin for extending the permission to want, but ultimately encouraging us to want Him most of all.

— RACHAEL ADAMS, host of the Love Offering Podcast

In the Waiting is insightful, creative, and deeply profound. There is a lot of waiting in the Bible. God makes many magnificent promises which often are fulfilled only after long years, even generations, of waiting. This study enters the stories of Biblical characters as they waited; sometimes in anticipation and joy, but sometimes also in suffering, confusion, and doubt. Jazmin weaves an informed, thoughtful, and reflective reading of each story, which leads the reader on a journey to ponder questions such as "What am I waiting for?" "How should I wait?" and "Where is God while I wait?" As you read this book, have your Bible open and your heart prepared to encounter God. He is with you even as you wait.

— MICHAEL SCHWIND, seminary student

This book is such a great guide through times of waiting. Jazmin points you towards Christ every step of the way. It has been so crucial to me in my own time of waiting!

— EVA KUBASIAK, creator of the *Deep Dive Journal*

For the waiting ones. For those who want and don't yet have. Those trusting the Lord for something they can't see. God is near. He is right here. Present in your waiting. May these pages help you press all the deeper into relationship with Him.

Get access to companion teaching videos for small groups or individual study and other bonuses at jazminnfrank.com/waiting.

Table of Contents

	Introduction	9
	Bible Study Skills	11
DAY 1:	Name Your Wait	15
DAY 2:	Creation: The Origin of Waiting	17
DAY 3:	Abram: Trusting God with the Details	21
DAY 4:	Noah: Working While You Wait	25
DAY 5:	Hagar: You Are Seen	29
DAY 6:	Sarah: Feeling Forgotten	33
DAY 7:	Rebekah: Don't Manipulate Your Wait	37
DAY 8:	Job: The God Who Takes and Gives	41
DAY 9:	Leah: New Desires	45
DAY 10:	Rachel: The Competition of Waiting	51
DAY 11:	Jacob: Shaped in the Waiting	55
DAY 12:	Joseph: Remain Faithful	59
DAY 13:	Israel: God is Still Working in the Silence	63
DAY 14:	Israel: One More Minute	67
DAY 15:	Israel: Remember God's Presence	71
DAY 16:	Caleb: When the Waiting Isn't Your Fault	75
DAY 17:	Rahab: The Hope and Grief of Waiting	79
DAY 18:	Gideon: Be Assured	83
DAY 19:	Hannah: Allowed to Want	87
DAY 20:	Ruth: Revived Hope	91
DAY 21:	David: Part of a Bigger Story	95

DAY 22:	Elijah: The Loneliness of Waiting	99
DAY 23:	Esther: A Time of Preparation	103
DAY 24:	Shadrach, Meshach, and Abednego: Stand Firm	107
DAY 25:	Jonah: Check Your Attitude	111
DAY 26:	Elizabeth and Zechariah: Perfect Timing	115
DAY 27:	Mary: Submitting to the Waiting	119
DAY 28:	Man at the Pool: Reset Your Hope	123
DAY 29:	Crowd of 5,000: Want the Right Thing	127
DAY 30:	Peter: Don't Get Distracted	131
DAY 31:	Mary and Martha: Sit With Jesus	135
DAY 32:	Zacchaeus: Seek Him Out	139
DAY 33:	The Bleeding Woman: The End of Yourself	143
DAY 34:	Mary of Bethany: Waiting and Grieving	147
DAY 35:	Jesus: Worth It	151
DAY 36:	Thomas: Room for Doubt	157
DAY 37:	The Disciples: Praying While You Wait	161
DAY 38:	Paul: Sufficient Grace	165
DAY 39:	New Creation: The End of Waiting	169
DAY 40:	Your Name Goes Here	173
	Leader Resources	175
	Acknowledgements	189
	A Note from the Author	191

Introduction

Some stories take longer to tell.

Wander around any library or bookstore and you'll see books of all sizes and lengths. Some stories are straightforward while others contain so many twists and turns that it takes pages upon pages—and sometimes even multiple books—to resolve everything.

That fact is not only true in the book world, but it is also true in our lives. There are some things that come about quickly and easily without much struggle. Then there are those other things that take time. Lots of time. Often it feels like too much time.

We call those the waiting seasons, and if you're like me, you are not a fan of waiting.

But what if I told you that waiting is actually a good thing? What if these seasons are actually opportunities?

If you just rolled your eyes or felt that little fire of anger flicker in your gut, stick with me. I know how hard it is to hear that waiting is a good thing when your heart feels torn in two from an unanswered longing. I'm not here to tell you that waiting is good because it helps build character or patience or something like that, though it definitely can. I'm saying that waiting is meant to be something good and holy, another avenue to build relationship with God even in times when everything around us looks barren and empty.

This study is all about flipping waiting on its head. Over the next forty days we're going to dig into stories in Scripture of those who waited and how they met God—or rather, how God met them—in the midst of their wanting. We're going to take a look at their struggle and their faith. We're going to pay attention to their attitudes. We're going to read about people who ran ahead of God, and people who waited faithfully. We're going to eavesdrop on their prayers and listen for God's answers. All with the goal, not of finding a formula to end our waiting, but to encounter the God who is with us in the waiting. Hopefully by the end of it, *wait* won't be a word that we despise. Instead, we might find that this word becomes an invitation to deeper relationship with God as we abide in Him, trust Him, and anticipate His movement.

I'm not sure what you're waiting for, dear heart. I don't know how long you've been waiting or how you feel about it, but you picked up this book for a reason, whether you chose it or it was given to you, and I want to ask you to enter into it vulnerably and honestly.

We're probably going to poke at some pain points, but don't run away. Allow yourself to enter into the pain, the disappointment, the bitterness, the resentment, the hopelessness, and invite God to enter into all of that honest emotion with you. Allow Him to minister to your hurting and weary heart. Allow Him to meet you in the waiting. And if I can give you one bit of encouragement before we begin, it's to go back to the statement I started with: Some stories just take time to tell. But often the stories with all the twists, turns, and waiting are the ones with the sweetest resolutions.

Because of the nature of this topic, it might be beneficial to gather a couple of other people to study with. If you're studying with a group, there is a leader guide in the back of this book. Teaching videos are also available to help you dive deeper into this topic of waiting. These videos are useful for both groups and individuals. You can access those videos and other bonus resources by visiting jazminnfrank.com/waiting.

Blessings on the journey, dear heart.

I pray you come out on the other side loving God more, loving His story more, and with a deeper understanding of what it looks like to live devoted to Him even in the waiting.

Live in His love,

Bible Study Skills

It's my personal goal in each study I create not just to feed you content, but to also teach you skills. Studying the Bible can feel like a daunting task, but anyone can do it. You don't need a degree or special training, just a few handy tools and a heart open to the leading of the Holy Spirit. So before we dive into the actual study, let's talk about a few skills that you can use to dig deep into Scripture, both in this study and in your personal Bible study time:

SKILL #1 ACTIVE READING

You make the move from Bible reading to Bible study when you actively engage in God's Word. This can happen in a lot of different ways like underlining, color coding, marking in the margins, or keeping a journal.

One great way I've found to easily engage is Scripture is to ask questions. I like to say that the Bible is God's way of inviting us into conversation with Him. Rather than passively reading Scripture, we can engage in God's Word by asking questions about what we read and how it applies to our lives.

Each day of this study, before I teach or share anything, I'm going to give you space to engage in God's Word yourself. You'll have the passage of Scripture and a block of space to respond to what you read. You can use this space in whatever way you'd like, but if I can encourage you to stretch your Bible study muscles just a bit, I want to challenge you to use this space to jot down questions and record whatever answers you find or receive from God. My Bible study group has three questions we ask every week. If you don't know what to ask, these three questions are great ones to use:

1. Where is God in this passage?
2. Who does God reveal Himself to be in this passage?
3. How might this passage help me in my own waiting?

These questions provide a great framework to make observations about what you read, pay attention to where God is and what He reveals about Himself, and apply what you read to your life.

SKILL #2 UNDERSTAND THE BIG PICTURE OF SCRIPTURE

Though the Bible is made up of 66 individual books, each book helps tell the overarching story of God. From Genesis to Revelation, God is the main character.

The beauty of this study is that we're not settling in to any particular book of the Bible. We're going to spend time in both the Old and New Testament, popping in and out of people's stories, but all of these stories—though they might seem separate—fit together to tell the greater story of God's plan to restore relationship between humanity and Himself. Studying Scripture gets a little easier when you have a grasp of how all of these stories tie together.

For the most part, this study is organized chronologically. This means the stories of the people we're going to study occur in the order they happened historically. You'll find as we move through these next forty days, some stories will be revisited often. Abraham's waiting, for example, is intimately connected to many other passages of Scripture because Abraham was waiting on God for something that stretched far beyond his own lifetime. Pay attention to how these stories connect. Remember, while we are going to focus on individual people, all of these stories help tell God's story.

SKILL #3 CHARACTER STUDY

A character study is when you take a person and focus on their struggles, their victories, their interactions with God, and how they grow in their faith. That's exactly what we're going to do here. Now you might be wondering, "Why should I spend time studying people's stories in the Bible, if it's really all about God?"

We should spend time studying their stories because we can learn a lot about God by paying attention to how He interacts with people.

We know God through His Word, yes, but not just through what He *says*. We learn a lot about God's character and His heart as we see how He *interacts* with people. By paying attention to those who have gone before us, we can learn from their mistakes, grow from their faith, and encounter God in new ways. We are people who learn from people and we have a lot to learn from the men and women of Scripture. They are no different from us, except that they are several generations removed. The people in Scripture are real with real histories. They had emotions, desires, secrets, scars. They were all humans in need of a Savior just as we are and we can stand to learn something from their experiences, choices, and perspectives.

One last thing to keep in mind as you read is to allow God to lead you. A simple moment of asking God to speak, to be present, will go far in helping you understand what you study and invest in your relationship with Him. So before we begin Day 1, let's pray together.

Lord, we invite you into this space. You have gone before us. You know what these pages hold and how we will encounter You over the next forty days. You know what we are waiting for and how we feel about it. You know what wounds the waiting has caused us. We ask that You would be near. We ask that Your Word would speak healing and hope to our hearts. We ask that we would hear Your voice, encounter Your presence, know You deeper, and love You more than when we began. You are God. You are Lord over our hearts, Lord over our desires, and Lord over the wanting seasons. Help us see You here, Lord. Help us know You better. And help us to desire You above all else.

Day 1: Name Your Wait

Before we dive into studying other people's stories, I want us to spend today looking at your own story. You picked up this study for a reason, most likely because you're in your own season of wanting and waiting. I know waiting seasons can be tender and touchy, but I want to give you some safe space to share your story here.

Don't feel like you have to write a novel. I'll guide you. Just a few words can help you name your wanting. Then on our last day of the study I'll ask you to revisit your story. Maybe by the end of the 40 days you will have seen some movement in your waiting. Maybe something will have changed, or maybe you will find yourself even deeper in the waiting. Whatever your circumstances look like, I hope that when we get to the end of this study you'll notice that something has changed in your heart.

My hope is that through this study you'll learn how to connect with God, that you will value Him not because of what He can give you, but because He gave up everything to have a relationship with you.

Take your time here. Be honest. Use this as your starting point to connect with God.

What are you waiting for?

What is your view of God in the waiting? Do you blame Him? Do you believe He'll come through?

IN THE WAITING

How long have you been waiting? When did the waiting start?

What answers or movement have you experienced in your waiting so far?

What are you hoping to glean from this study?

What verses, words, songs, stories, or images have been encouraging to you in your waiting?

Best case scenario, what do you hope God will do over the next forty days?

Day 2: The Origin of Waiting

Creation

GENESIS 1:1-3:7

In the beginning God created the heavens and the earth. Now the earth was formless and empty, darkness covered the surface of the watery depths, and the Spirit of God was hovering over the surface of the waters. (Genesis 1:1-2)

The first two verses in Genesis might just be some of my favorite in all of Scripture. Do you know why? Maybe you caught it too? It's because of this sense of anticipation.

Before Creation even existed, this open expanse of nothingness seemed to hold its breath—ready and waiting, expecting something grand to happen.

And it did! Light, sky, night, day, land, sea, sun, moon, stars. All of it God breathed into existence with the words "Let there be" and after each act of creation, He declared it good. God's tongue spun the entire universe into being, giving way to a deep and satisfying exhale for that anticipatory inhale. No longer was the Spirit of God simply hovering. He was moving, breathing life into a world that hadn't existed before.

Then to top off His creation song, God makes man and woman and calls them good too. He establishes relationship with them and every day He met with them in the cool of the evening. It was a meeting and a conversation, a time when humanity simply enjoyed being in their Creator's presence. It was a time that they came to anticipate. They waited for it. They expected it.

So often in our modern language, the word "wait" has negative emotions tied to it.

When you think of the word *wait* what emotions or feelings rise up?

Wait for many of us feels like a bad four-letter word. It means we're being deprived of something or pushed aside, our desires unmet. At least for me, waiting is often connected with fear that the thing I'm waiting for won't actually happen.

The word *wait* often feels like a no.

DAY 2: THE ORIGIN OF WAITING

But here in the context of Creation *wait* has a beautiful sense of expectancy. The Spirit hovered. All of that nothingness held its breath, waiting, and then life sprang out of nowhere!

Adam and Eve tended to the garden, cared for the creatures, nurtured their relationship with each other, all the while knowing that their Father would show up when the evening became cool and the sun started its watercolor descent. They waited for Him, but there was no fear of being denied. They expected good things from God, they expected Him to show up, and their expectations were met because in those sacred moments in Eden, everything was as it should be.

The relationship between God and humanity was as it should be. They never doubted Him to show up or take care of them. But all of that surety, dissolved when the serpent whispered doubt into Eve's ear for the first time. His line of questioning left Eve wondering, "Is God really good?"

The moment Eve took and ate of the Tree of Knowledge of Good and Evil and handed it to Adam, both of them decided that God wasn't good. They stopped expecting good things from Him and decided He was holding out on them. They took and ate and in that moment their beautiful, expectant world was flipped on its head. Creation was no longer whole or expectant of God's goodness.

I think one of the reasons waiting is so hard is because the same doubt that crept in with Eve's bite of that fruit is now hardwired into us. We struggle to believe that God is good to us and we stop expecting good things from Him.

Do you believe God is good? The "church answer" to that is "yes, of course!" But let's set aside the church answers for a moment and settle into this waiting space. Do *you* believe God is good and kind right here in your waiting? How do you feel about Him? Do you feel like He's listening to you or aware of what you're feeling in this season? Or do you feel slighted, ignored, or unimportant to Him?

If we're going to allow these seasons of wanting and waiting to draw us closer to God, our first step is to remember who God really is and to ask Him to awaken our hearts to His goodness.

It's time to press back into the original intent of waiting and wait with expectancy, not for the object of our wait, but for God to show up and move.

It's time to expect God's goodness smack dab in the middle of our waiting.

It's time to remind our broken, busted, and bruised hearts that God is good, that He can be trusted, and that we can expect good things from Him.

You know what else happened that day the serpent slithered in? Someone else entered a season of waiting.

IN THE WAITING

Read Genesis 3:22-24. Whose waiting started and what was that person waiting for?

Waiting can feel isolated and lonely. Depending on what you're waiting for, it may even feel like no one else in your community quite understands what you're going through. But God does. That day when He sent Adam and Eve out of Eden, God began to wait for the time when sin would be eliminated from the world He had created, and relationship with humanity would be restored.

In the waiting we can trust God's goodness. We can expect good things from Him. And we can rest in the truth that God is familiar with the ache of wanting.

Have you ever considered that God is waiting? How does that truth help you draw closer to Him?

Day 3: Trusting God with the Details

Abram

GENESIS 12:1-9

Like Bilbo Baggins leaving the Shire in *The Hobbit* and setting off on his grand adventure, following God into something new can be exciting. We may ask God to do something in our lives, or we may feel Him speaking something new over us. This beginning stage of waiting in faith can be a time full of joy and anticipation. We're excited about what God will do and we're fully expecting Him to work.

Abram, whose name would later be changed to Abraham, faced an interesting such a call to something new: "Go...to the land that I will show you" (Genesis 12:1). God didn't provide exact coordinates of the destination. He didn't give Abram the name of the town he would eventually call home. God just said go, and Abram had to trust God to lead him.

Nowhere in today's passage do we see Abram questioning God—not when He calls Abram away from his home and his family, not when God promises this old man and his barren wife a child, and not when God promises to make Abram into a nation through whom the whole world would be blessed.

Abram believes it all and he goes, willingly following God into the unknown.

God is a detail-oriented God. We saw that a few days ago in Genesis 1 when God creates the universe. Every detail is shared. We'll see that later in Exodus when God gives Israel the Law and all the minute details of living a holy life are outlined for the people. But just because God knows all the details doesn't mean He *shares* all of them with us.

Part of the purpose of waiting seasons is to draw us into deeper relationship and deeper reliance upon God. If I have all the details of the wait—if I know where I'm going, how I'll get there, and all the obstacles I'll face along the way—I'm prone to speed on ahead of God and do life on my own. Or, depending on the details, I may run in the complete opposite direction because the journey ahead looks too intimidating, too impossible, too scary.

Withholding details may seem unkind on God's part, but it's actually one of the kindest things He could do because it keeps us from running scared and invites us to rely on Him. When we are able to respond like Abram and settle into the waiting and trust that God knows where He's leading us even if we don't know, there is freedom to be found in the waiting.

You know what else is really neat about God's relationship with Abram? Though when God calls Abram He gives him very little detail, God slowly reveals things as they go.

Read verses 7-9 again. What other details does God reveal to Abram and how does Abram respond to this new information?

DAY 3: TRUSTING GOD WITH THE DETAILS

Along the journey God meets Abram multiple times and when that happens, Abram sets up alters, marking the places where God speaks and reveals His presence. Abram also made space to seek God on his own. With or without new information, Abram made his relationship with God and his worship of God his priority. Long before God delivered on what He promised, Abram made the effort to draw near to God.

Let's approach our waiting with the same kind of faith Abram had—the kind of faith that is willing to wait on details and follow God obediently even when we don't know how things will play out along the way. Let's allow God to cultivate within us a heart that trusts His leading even when it feels like we're following blind. Let's choose to have a heart that worships and seeks God during every leg of the journey. Let's prioritize our relationship with Him even while we're waiting on what He's promised.

What details do you wish you knew about your waiting?

In what way do you see God's kindness in not letting you in on all of the details?

How can you prioritize your relationship with God?

Day 4: Working While You Wait

Noah

GENESIS 6:9-22

I really enjoy time lapses in movies. We get the gist of time passing, but not the details of what happens between the plot points. Time lapses keep the story moving.

Sometimes Scripture uses time lapses too. The author gives us the big details they want us to focus on, and often that makes us feel like things happen pretty quickly. One simple sentence can move us ahead in time by days, months, or even years.

Take another look at verse 22 from today's reading: "And Noah did this. He did everything that God had commanded him."

Pretty great, right? God gave instructions, and Noah faithfully obeyed, completing everything the Lord had told him. Good job, Noah!

But can we take a moment to remember what exactly it was God asked Noah to do?

In your own words, summarize God's instructions to Noah.

God told Noah that the earth had become corrupt and that He was going to send a flood to wipe out all life and start over with just Noah and his family. In order to be saved from the flood, God instructed Noah to build a huge, multi-leveled boat, gather two of every kind of animal and bird, and gather enough food for his family and all the animals.

This was no small task and it took decades to complete! Noah is 500 years old when we meet him as the father of three sons (Genesis 5:32), and we learn that he is 600 when the flood begins (Genesis 7:6). That's a hundred years between when we meet Noah and when the fulfillment of God's word about the flood comes. 100 years of waiting! Several decades of sawing, hammering, building, and painting with pitch. 100 years of planting, harvesting crops, storing goods, tending to animals, and dealing with the jeers of his community as Noah prepared for a flood in the desert.

Often when we think of waiting we picture sitting there twiddling our thumbs, doing nothing. Waiting has a sort of idleness connected to it. Noah's season of waiting, however, was not marked by idleness. He had work to do. Noah is remembered for his faithfulness to the Lord because he did the work God had given him to do while he waited for that flood to arrive.

I wonder if Noah ever doubted God's word. By year 57 was he wondering if maybe he really was a fool like his neighbors said? Did he think he was wasting all of his time and gopher

DAY 4: WORKING WHILE YOU WAIT

wood? I wouldn't put it past him for having his days of doubt—he was human, after all—but on those days he did doubt and question, he did not waiver in his work. Noah waited well by working obediently.

Waiting well doesn't always mean that we sit there and do nothing. Sometimes God gives us work to do while we wait. Maybe it's not a building project like the one He gave to Noah, but maybe your heart needs tending to. Maybe plans need to be prepared or relationships need mended. Maybe that resume needs revamped or that skill honed. Maybe your work is simply to trust God in the waiting.

Whatever it is, work faithfully as you watch to see how God comes through. Allow that work to be your way of connecting and staying in tune with the Lord.

What work has God given you in this season of waiting? Is there any work He's given you that you've been avoiding? How might doing that good work help you wait well?

What hope can you glean from Noah's waiting?

Day 5: You Are Seen

Hagar

GENESIS 16:1-16

IN THE WAITING

Sometimes when the waiting stretches on, we seek our own solutions. *God's not doing His job, so I'm going to take control.* I'm guilty of this more than I'd like to admit.

That's the point Sarai, Abram's wife, reached in today's passage. It had been ten years since God first promised Abram land and descendants, and while he was wandering about the land, his wife remained barren. After years of waiting she decided to take matters into her own hands.

Culture dictated that if a woman couldn't bear her own children, she could offer a servant to her husband as a second wife and surrogate mother, so that's what Sarai does. We don't know the reasoning behind Sarai's action. Perhaps she never believed that God's promise that Abram would have children involved her. Or perhaps she had just given up after a lifetime of waiting. Whatever her reasons, Sarai gives her maidservant Hagar to Abram as a wife, and when Hagar became pregnant things got complicated. Hagar wasn't just Sarai's lowly Egyptian servant anymore. In fact, she was able to do something her mistress couldn't. Hagar, not Sarai, would give birth to Abram's firstborn child.

You've heard the expression "Hurt people, hurt people." How did Sarai's actions effect Hagar?

Like a bad soap opera, the drama between these two women escalates until Sarai has had enough of Hagar's contempt and Hagar has had enough of Sarai's mistreatment. So, Hagar runs. Pregnant, poor, and without a plan, she ends up at a well in the middle of nowhere. She hadn't asked for this. She'd been caught in the middle of Sarai's scheming to end her own waiting, and now Hagar has been ushered into the middle of her own. Feeling alone, unwanted, and unseen, she is desperate for relief.

It's there at the well, in Hagar's moment of desperation that God shows up. He urges her to return and submit to Sarai, but He also offers a blessing. God tells her about the son she carries in her womb. Hagar and her son Ishmael become part of this promise of a multitude that would come from Abram's descendants. The moment was so impactful that Hagar names the place where she met God, and she calls Him the "God who sees me." And her child's name, Ishmael, would be a constant reminder that God hears.

Our God is a God who sees and hears.

Waiting has a way of blinding our eyes to God's presence and His provision. We can become so focused on our circumstances and our lack and our struggles that we miss out on the fact that God is right there. He is fully aware of what is happening and He is ready to open our eyes to His presence.

Perhaps one of the most comforting ways we can draw near to God is simply by remembering that God sees and hears us. Nothing has escaped His notice. You are not alone. You are not abandoned. God sees you right where you are.

In what ways do you feel unseen in your waiting?

What hope have you found in Hagar's story today?

Day 6: Feeling Forgotten

Sarah

GENESIS 17:15-21, 18:1-15

After yesterday's lesson on Hagar, I feel like God is on a roll with using names as reminders of what He's doing in people's lives. Hagar's son was given the name Ishmael to be a reminder that God sees and hears. Now Abraham and Sarah's promised child, Isaac, is given a name that means laughter and joy, and that's exactly what little Isaac would bring to his parents after so many years of waiting.

When Abraham first received God's promise that a nation would come from him and that God would provide land for all of Abraham's future descendants, I always imagine Sarah being privy to that promise. She is, after all, Abraham's wife. If Abraham is going to have children, she's going to be the one to bear them. We learn in Genesis 11:30 that she is barren, but I'm certain God's word to Abraham stirred up hope in Sarah. Her long held desire of holding a child in her arms would be fulfilled. God would do it. She just had to wait and watch it happen. So she followed her husband into this new life, all the while waiting for God's promise to unfold.

Then all of that drama happened with Hagar and it seemed like Sarah has given up hope. Her plan to have a child through her maidservant didn't pan out quite like she'd hoped. It seems God's promise wasn't for her after all, or so she thinks as she slips quietly into the background of the story until God speaks up again.

What I love so much about Sarah's story is the lengths God goes to remind Sarah that her waiting is just a season, and that He hasn't forgotten about her. This time when God reminds Abraham of this promised child, the heir that would carry on the covenant, God also clearly states that Sarah will bear that child. Then He goes one step further to make sure Sarah hears the promise for herself. Up until chapter 18 Sarah has been waiting on a second-hand promise, but God shows up and allows her to overhear His plans with her own ears.

Reread Genesis 18:9-15. How can you tell that this visit of the men at Abraham's tent is for Sarah's benefit?

When Sarah hears God's plans, she laughs. Truly it's impossible at this point, she thinks. Biologically. Emotionally. It all just feels like a cruel joke, and she's past the point of being sad. Now, the promise just feels laughable. How could she, a barren woman well past the peak of life, have ever believed this promise of a child was for her?

Mid-laugh, God calls her out and speaks the promise again, putting a time stamp on it: "I will certainly come back to you *in a year's time,* and your wife Sarah will have a son." (18:10,

DAY 6: FEELING FORGOTTEN

emphasis added). One year later Sarah gives birth to a baby boy, just as the heavenly visitor had said, and she calls him Isaac.

When we're waiting on God to do something He said He would do, but time keeps passing without any progress, it can be easy to feel like God has forgotten about us. Natural deadlines pass us by while friends and family members and complete strangers on social media are experiencing the very things we've begged and believed God for. But God hasn't forgotten. He may not give you that thing you're waiting for in the time or way you imagine, but He has not forgotten you. If He promised, He will be faithful to come through on His word.

Look up Hebrews 10:24. How does this verse relate to today's lesson?

The Lord is our source of hope. No matter what, we can trust His character. He will come through, and until He does, you can trust that God hears every prayer and plea. He catches every tear your hurting heart has birthed. He is well acquainted with your longing. Things might look impossible right now, but turn your ear to God. Hear Him calling you "child" and "beloved." Those are not names of the forgotten. Those are the names bestowed upon one who is loved by the One who is Love. Like Sarah, one day your season of waiting will pass and you will once again be filled with laughter and joy.

In what areas of your life do you feel forgotten?

What do you need from God today to help you in your waiting?

IN THE WAITING

How do you feel about the fact that God calls you "child" and beloved?" How do those names encourage you in your waiting?

Day 7: Don't Manipulate Your Wait

Rebekah

GENESIS 25:19-26, 27:1-17

IN THE WAITING

Waiting often begins with a promise—or at the very least a hope, a desire that God would do something. For Rebekah, she had a very clear word from God. During a hard pregnancy, after a season of barrenness, Rebekah turns to the Lord and asks why the baby inside her is wreaking such havoc on her body.

God spoke to her and told her two things. First, He told her that she wasn't just carrying one baby, but two. Twins. The other He told her was a hint about the future of those baby boys.

What information did God give to Rebekah about her babies?

Perhaps God's insight in the lives of her children was the reason Rebekah became so fond of Jacob. She took God's word to heart; she believed Him when He said that the older brother would serve the younger brother. But then she tried to take matters into her own hands. If there is one consistency we've seen in the stories we've studied so far, it's that waiting tends to get more complicated and last longer when we try to work out our own end to the story.

What was Rebekah's plan for Jacob?

In that culture, the older son had the power, and a lot of that power came from the bulk of their father's inheritance. The oldest son carried special privileges and received a double portion of the blessing passed on by his father. But God told Rebekah, before the twins were born, that the younger son was the one who would be blessed. Thinking only of earthly things, Rebekah set about to make sure that blessing came to Jacob. After all, God had promised this, right?

Sometimes we can take what God has promised, or the hope we have about what He might do, and we twist it. We are human and we have limited understanding, but more often than

DAY 7: DON'T MANIPULATE YOUR WAIT

not we like to think we know exactly how and when things will happen.

Rebekah thought she knew how this would play out. Instead of waiting on God to show her what the womb-promise meant, Rebekah hatched a scheme for Jacob to pose as his brother Esau and trick Isaac into bestowing the blessing of the firstborn onto Jacob. The plan, while it succeeded in getting Jacob the blessing meant for his older brother, also sent him on the run for his life.

Read Genesis 27:41-46. How did Rebekah's schemes affect Jacob and the rest of her family?

I wonder how things might have been different had Rebekah waited on God to raise Jacob up instead of trying to catapult him there with her plotting.

We need to be careful in the waiting not to pull a Rebekah—to take a word from the Lord and run ahead of Him, seeking to bring it about ourselves. The more I learn about God and His ways, the more I see just how much I don't understand about how He works. He is faithful to His word, but we can take it to mean something different than He intended. We can get so caught up in how it will happen that we forget that God already has a plan. The best way to navigate seasons of waiting, no matter how long they stretch on, is to press deeper into relationship with God and believe that He knows what He's doing. We also need to recognize, as we'll see later in Jacob's story, that God's plan is often far greater than whatever we think we'll get by trying to end the waiting ourselves.

Have you ever tried to bring about God's plans on your own? How did that work out?

IN THE WAITING

Take some time today to surrender the outcome of your wait to the Lord. Acknowledge that this may not play out like you expect, but commit to trusting Him, His timing, and His ways no matter what.

Day 8: The God Who Takes and Gives

Job

JOB 1:1-22

There was a year in my recent history where I spent a good chunk of time in the book of Job. A little too much time if you ask me. It was a year when things had just kind of blown up and I was looking for answers. For relief. For God. I needed to know where He was in that hard season, and where else do you go to find God in the midst of suffering besides the book of Job?

Job was a godly man, righteous, and blameless. He sought the Lord. He made sacrifices on behalf of his children, in case they had committed any sins against God. He was just a good dude. Then, all hell broke loose—all of his wealth was taken from him and his children were killed.

I'm amazed that in the midst of such immense loss, Job is brought to his knees not only in sorrow and grief, but also in worship. All of his wealth, most of his family, the legacy that would have been carried on through his children, his workers—all of it was lost. If I were in Job's shoes my first thought would not have been worship but a long, loud, mournful, "Why, God?!" I would have blamed Him. I would have shaken my fist at the heavens.

But Job responds differently. Look at verses 20-22 again:

"Then Job stood up, tore his robe, and shaved his head. He fell to the ground and worshiped saying: Naked I came from my mother's womb, and naked I will leave this life. The Lord gives and the Lord takes away. Blessed be the name of the Lord. Throughout all this Job did not sin or blame God for anything" (verses 20-22).

Job faced a lot of loss in a very short amount of time. In what ways do you think your response to God would have been different to Job's?

Because of how the book of Job begins, we know the reason for Job's suffering. Satan is trying to prove a point—that Job's faithfulness to God is based solely on the fact that Job has a good life. He's blessed, so of course he serves God faithfully. God decides to let Satan test out his theory. In some ways I want to call that unfair. Why put Job through the ringer? God didn't cause it, but He certainly allowed it. Why would God allow so much suffering?

That is the age old question isn't it? How could a good God could let His people suffer?

I ask that question in my own waiting. Some seasons of waiting are shorter and kinder than others, but for those seasons that feel more like suffering than hopeful expectation, whether internal or circumstantial, it can be easy to give into the grief and blame God. It can be tempting to point our finger at God and angrily declare all of this as His fault, to give into the belief that He isn't kind and doesn't actually care about us.

What I love about Job, though, and the thing I think we can learn from him, is that Job remained faithful and he kept his relationship with God open. The man could have walked away and denied God. That was what Satan wanted. That was what Job's wife wanted when she told him to curse God and die. Instead, Job stayed, he voiced his pain, he asked God questions, and he acknowledged God's sovereignty—His supreme rule over Job's life.

"The Lord gives and the Lord takes away, blessed be the name of the Lord."

Even in the midst of grief, Job gives all authority to God. He can do as He pleases, and just because God chooses to take—or withhold or tell us to wait—instead of giving us what we want, we have no less reason to praise Him. In fact, I think we have even *more* reason to praise Him.

There are some seasons of waiting that feel heavy and are marked by disappointment, brokenness, and perhaps even tragedy. That thing we're waiting for keeps eluding us. Perhaps it was even within our grasp when everything turned to dust and fell through our fingers, causing the wait to stretch on.

But even in those seasons can we, like Job, come before God with a heart of worship?

Worship is easy when we're getting, but learning how to worship and praise the Lord when He chooses not to give, that's where it really matters. Because it's at that point our hearts are put to the test. Will we stick with God no matter what, or are we just trying to get something from Him? Learning how to worship God in any and every season takes our focus off that thing we're waiting for and places it back in the rightful place: on our loving Father who knows best and loves us more than we can understand. And sometimes being a good parent means saying no, taking instead of giving, or saying wait.

Whether He's giving, taking, or asking that we wait, can we worship Him? Can we trust God enough—even just a mustard seed ounce of faith—to believe that His answer is good?

Do you view God as more of a taker or a giver? How has that affected your relationship with Him?

IN THE WAITING

How can you worship Him here in the waiting? Take some time to do that now. Write out a prayer of praise, lift your hands and speak it out loud, sing the Lord a song. Let worship be your focus today.

Day 9: New Desires

Leah

GENESIS 29:1-35

IN THE WAITING

Loneliness is a form of waiting. We're waiting for someone to turn their head in our direction, to pay attention and show us that we matter to them, that we're worth investing in. Loneliness is something Leah is well acquainted with. She knows how it feels to be passed over, especially when compared to her younger sister Rachel.

In all possible ways, Leah is seen as the lesser sister in appearance and marriageability. When Jacob comes to town and starts paying attention to Rachel, their father Laban hatches a scheme. Scheming seems to run in this family, because, did you happen to catch that Laban is Rebekah's brother? So when Jacob flees from Esau, he goes to his uncle's house, and while there he notices Rachel. Jacob agrees to work seven years in exchange for Rachel's hand in marriage, but when the seven years are up and Leah still hasn't been married off to anyone, Laban marries Leah off to Jacob, her wedding veil hiding the fact that she is not Jacob's expected bride, Rachel. When Jacob wakes up the next morning to find Leah beside him instead of Rachel, he is furious.

Leah's father works out another deal with Jacob so that he gets Rachel in exchange for another seven years of work. Not only does Leah have to continue to live under the shadow of her younger, better-looking sister, but now she must also share a husband.

Step into Leah's shoes (or sandals). Is there any way you find yourself connecting with her particular brand of waiting?

My heart aches for Leah. She desperately wants someone to love her.

And Someone does.

In verse 31 we see God's love poured out on Leah when He enables her to bear a child. His love gives her the gift of loving another. However, Leah is too blind, too caught up in her own wanting to see it. When the child is born, a son, she calls him Reuben and says, "The Lord has seen my affliation; surely my husband will love me now" (verse 32b).

We've talked in previous lessons about how in that culture a woman's worth was based in her ability to bear sons. Rachel might have everything else going for her, but she was barren. Perhaps Leah thought her wait for love was over. She was the wife with the child, and not just any child, but a son! This son would be Jacob's heir. Of course Jacob would take notice of her now.

DAY 9: NEW DESIRES

According to the rest of the passage, however, Leah's wait continued. She became pregnant with two more sons, Simeon and Levi, both of the boys bearing names declaring her desire for love. But by the time her fourth son Judah is born, something has changed in Leah's heart.

What does Judah's name mean?

This is one of those places in Scripture where I wish we had more information. In a matter of three verses we see time passing. Leah carries three babies to term and no mention is given about how much time passed between pregnancies, but we're definitely dealing with years here. Years of Leah longing for the love of her husband until finally, at Judah's birth, she stops grasping for her husband's attention and praises God for what she does have.

It took a long time, but I believe part of the hidden beauty of Leah's story, a beauty we can see if we allow ourselves to settle in between the lines and in the unstated things of Scripture, is that somewhere along the way God moved in Leah's heart. It wasn't all at once. From the time she started having children to the time she wasn't able to anymore, God was moving in Leah's heart and redirecting her wants—redirecting her gaze up from her own loneliness to recognize the love of her Father that she's had all along.

As hard as it is for us to see clearly in the middle of desperate wanting, sometimes we experience seasons of waiting because God is reshaping our hearts to want something else.

Flip over to Psalm 37:3-6. How does this passage relate to Leah's story?

Leah's desire for her husband's love wasn't sinful. It makes sense for a wife to want to be loved by her husband. However, Leah's desire for love ran deep. *Unloved* was a label attached to her identity and the love of a husband wouldn't fix that level of pain. No, the only kind of love that could do that is the love of the One who knitted Leah together in her mother's womb. God was willing to play the long game with Leah in order for her to learn just how much she was loved by Him.

IN THE WAITING

As far as we know, Leah never got what she wanted. Rachel remained the favorite wife. But I think Leah got something far better. She got to experience the love of her Father.

Sometimes our waiting doesn't turn out like we hope it will. Like Leah, we may not receive what we're waiting for, and that's a hard reality; but that doesn't make God any less good. When He chooses not to do the thing you're waiting on, when His answer is no, look up and pay attention to what He *is* doing, and where He *is* working. Leah didn't win the love of her husband, but she was blessed with four children to love on, and more importantly, she found contentment in the Lord—at least for a short time. Keep reading in Genesis and you'll find that the rivalry between Leah and Rachel continues. Thus is the way of our wayward human hearts. We need constant training in what it looks like to live loved by God. But even there, grace can be found. God will go to immeasurable lengths to prove to us just how much we are loved.

Trust God, dear heart. We're going to keep saying that. Trust that God will do what's best for you even if that means you don't end up with what you're waiting on. Trust that if God's in control—and He is—you'll end up with something better than what you thought you were waiting on. Trust Him to plant new desires in your heart and commit your way to Him.

In what ways does your waiting make you feel overlooked?

How might God be using this wait to teach you something about Him or yourself?

DAY 9: NEW DESIRES

Are there any places where your identity has gotten wrapped up in that thing you're waiting for? Confess that and ask God to remind you of your true identity as His beloved child.

Day 10: The Competition of Waiting

Rachel

GENESIS 30:1-24

IN THE WAITING

Yesterday we focused on Leah's waiting, but today we'll turn our attention to Rachel. Though the two sisters are described as being drastically different in appearance, Rachel and Leah have more in common than perhaps they want to admit. Caught in a competition for the love of their husband and in their desire for children, both women know what it is to want and not have.

We need look no further than our own hearts to see that sometimes in the waiting, competition sinks in deep. We watch those around us, strangers and friends, gaining the thing we want—a baby, a spouse, a job, a place to call home, a community, a dream-achieved. We watch them win and we feel like we're losing, like somehow we just can't keep up.

Just like Rachel has the one thing Leah wants—the love of her husband—Leah has something Rachel wants—children.

The sisters begin this all-out war in child-bearing. Rachel sees her sister pulling ahead, already caring for four children, while Rachel's arms remain empty. She goes to Jacob and complains, blaming him for her barrenness.

Describe the interaction between Rachel and Jacob.

Perhaps it seems a little dramatic, but anyone who has been waiting a long time only to find someone else being blessed in that area, can begin to feel a little desperate. We see this with Rachel as she casts blame and makes demands. Suddenly this isn't just about expecting God to move in a particular way. It's become a competition, and Rachel is desperate to catch up lest she lose to her sister.

Jacob passes the blame for Rachel's childlessness back to God: "Am I in the place of God? He has withheld offspring from you!" (verse 2). His response is harsh and definitely not sympathetic, but I'm not sure I can blame Jacob. He's found himself in the middle of a war between his sister-wives. It's a situation he never asked to be in, but his father-in-law threw him into when Laban tricked Jacob into marrying both of his daughters.

Utilizing the same cultural expectation Sarah used when she gave Hagar as a wife to her husband, Rachel offers her maidservant to Jacob as a wife and surrogate mother. Finally she's in the running of bearing children. Finally she's catching up to her sister.

I can just imagine what life felt like in that home. Jacob's family is growing, but his wives are feuding, and both women are lost in their wanting.

DAY 10: THE COMPETITION OF WAITING

Something in Rachel's heart, though, is wrestling with God. When we're caught in the waiting and everyone else seems to be moving on ahead, we are bound to wrestle a bit with God. And sometimes that wrestling with God, as in Rachel's case, turns into wrestling with other people as well. Bitterness and that feeling of competition can run rampant through our veins. We may work out our own way to end the waiting. We find a way to do something so that it feels like we're catching up, but the reality is there is only one way the waiting ends.

Look at verse 22 again. Why did Rachel's wait end? What happened?

The word *remember* here isn't used the same way we modern day readers understand it. God didn't forget Rachel and suddenly remember that He fell behind in giving her children. No, *remember* in Scripture, especially when God is the one doing the remembering, is all about taking action.

When God remembers, He is ready to move and make something happen. When the Bible says that God remembers, that is the point where the waiting ends and God comes through.

Rachel's desire for children was never far from God's mind. He knew her heart; He knew her ache. He allowed this little competition to play out between Rachel and her sister; but when God finally answers and Rachel gives birth to her firstborn son, Rachel gives credit to God.

What does Rachel say after Joseph is born?

God, not Rachel's attempts to keep up with her sister, was the one who took away her disgrace and lifted up her heart. And it's on the tail of Joseph's birth that Rachel turns again to God and asks for another child. She doesn't demand her husband sleep with her. She doesn't offer up another servant wife. She doesn't flaunt her child in front of her sister. Perhaps her request is still based in competition, but I like to think that in the days following Joseph's birth, as she marveled at this child born of her own body, Rachel turned a hopeful heart back toward God and asked Him to do it again because He had proven Himself faithful.

Competition won't get us anywhere in the waiting. From my experience, it only stirs up anxiety, bitterness, jealousy, and creates a rift in relationships. It also robs us of the joy and anticipation we can find when our hearts are set on the faithfulness of God.

If you're caught in a season of waiting and you're looking around only to find others who are getting the thing you want, let me encourage you to take a deep breath. Let it out slowly. Refocus your gaze on God. He hasn't forgotten you. Keep wrestling with Him. Trust His timing. Allow your gaze to settle on Him and trust that He will remember you, just as He remembered to Rachel.

What part of your waiting feels like a competition right now?

Are there any relationships where the competition of waiting has caused a rift? What might you do to restore that relationship?

How can you find encouragement in Rachel's story to turn a hopeful heart back to God?

Day 11: Shaped by Waiting

Jacob

GENESIS 25:27-34, 28:10-22

Jacob is an interesting character. When Jacob is born, he's given a name which means "grasper" because, when he follows his twin brother out of the womb, Jacob is grasping Esau's heel. The wrestling match that started in the womb—the one that caused Rebekah to cry out to the Lord in the middle of the night—intensifies as the boys grow into men. Jacob continues to live up to his name, grasping at the birthright and blessing meant for Esau. Jacob lies and manipulates and deceives, and ends up running for his life from his infuriated brother.

While making his escape to his uncle's house, Jacob encounters God. Suddenly that word God gave to Rebekah, about how the older would serve the younger and the younger would be blessed, begins to make sense. Jacob's blessing was never about a physical inheritance from his father. It was about being included in God's covenant that began with Abraham.

Think back to our earlier lessons. What covenant did God make with Abraham?

Jacob is a continuation of Abraham's family line, his grandson. Now, God passes the same blessing on to Jacob: "I will give you and your offspring the land on which you are lying. Your offspring will be like the dust of the earth...All the peoples on earth will be blessed through you and your offspring" (Genesis 28:13-15).

The promise of blessing and covenant also comes with a promise of protection. The next day, before Jacob sets out from Bethel, he makes a promise to God in return.

Look at verses 18-22 again. What does Jacob promise God?

Jacob's wait begins that day. He promises to serve God faithfully, but Jacob is waiting to see if God will prove trustworthy, if He will do what He's promised. That encounter at Bethel changes Jacob and we see that change more clearly in the way he handles the whole Rachel and Leah situation. When Laban deceives Jacob and tricks Jacob into marrying both of his daughters, I feel like the old Jacob—the pre-Bethel Jacob—might have responded

DAY 11: SHAPED IN THE WAITING

differently. I imagine him shaking an angry fist or hatching some scheme to run off with Rachel, while leaving Leah in the dust. Instead he shows himself, surprisingly, to be a man of integrity. Obviously he has been wronged and he demands Laban make it right, but instead of pushing his own agenda, Jacob agrees to Laban's new terms of seven additional years so that he can have Rachel as a wife too.

As the years pass, we continue to see God's transforming work in Jacob's life.

Read Genesis 30:25-43. As Jacob's story continues, how do you see evidence of God's work in Jacob's life?

Though Jacob had been cheated, God blessed his work and used Laban's deception as an avenue of blessing as well. Jacob's flocks and herds increased. He prospered. His family grew. He came out of that season more richly blessed than he originally would have. Beyond his material blessings, Jacob's character also grew in those years. He got a taste of the same medicine from Laban that Jacob had offered his brother Esau, and even his father Isaac, but instead of running away, Jacob stuck around and came out better for it.

I wonder how often over those years Jacob served in Laban's house that God's covenant came back to him. How often did he remember God's promise to him and his promise to God? Did Jacob notice God's faithfulness as it was happening, or was it only in hindsight that he saw God's goodness in holding up His end of the bargain?

Waiting is rarely something we desire to enter into willingly, but these seasons can become powerful tools that God can use to shape, mold, and transform us. Instead of fighting the waiting, let's enter into it. Let's embrace the waiting for all it is and allow God to shape us and mold us and prepare us for what's next. Rather than trying to get out of the waiting, let's remain in the waiting and find God's blessing right there.

Looking back at the wait so far, how have you seen God bless you and grow your character?

IN THE WAITING

What encouragement for your own season of waiting do you find in Jacob's story?

Day 12: Remain Faithful

Joseph

GENESIS 37:1-11, 41:46-57, 45:1-14

Joseph's story is a long one, covering the last thirteen chapters of the book of Genesis, but his story begins with a dream—two dreams actually. Bundles of wheat and celestial bodies symbolize Joseph and his family as he stands at the center and they all bow down to him. Befuddled or excited by the dreams, he shares them with his brothers, who are already jealous of him because he is the favorite son of their father. Hearing Joseph's dreams and the implications that one day they would bow down before him and he would rule over them, pushes the brothers over the edge.

When an opportunity arises, Joseph's brothers dump him in a pit with the intent of killing him. They later decide to sell him into slavery. They get him and his ridiculous dreams out of the way and make a profit off of him too. Double win.

Joseph, however, suffers a great loss. He's deceived by his brothers, sent away from his father, and forced into slavery in a foreign land. To make matters worse, he ends up wrongly accused and then thrown into prison for something he never did.

So much for those dreams of leadership.

From Joseph's view in the prison cell, things probably looked pretty bleak. If those dreams he had as a teenager were indeed hints from God about what was the come, how in the world would those dreams come about? And how did he know those dreams weren't the result of some figs that just didn't agree with him? If we could ask Joseph what he was thinking during that time in prison, it's likely he would share numerous doubts and frustrations about how his life had turned out.

Yet on this side of the story, we know God is working. Over and over again throughout Joseph's journey we find him faithfully serving the Lord despite his horrendous circumstances, and the Lord continues to bless Joseph. Eventually, Joseph ends up exactly where the dreams prophesied: standing as a ruling authority over his brothers as they bow before him.

Sometimes our waiting begins with a desire, something we want. Other times, the waiting we find ourselves in is because God has spoken something to us and we're waiting for Him to bring it to pass. What makes the waiting really difficult, however, is when our circumstances end up looking completely opposite of what we believed God told us they would look like.

It may seem cruel for God to give Joseph those dreams as a teen when they wouldn't be realized for a few decades, but I wonder if maybe those dreams were actually a special grace from God. I wonder if God gave Joseph a promise he could hang onto throughout his journey—a sign that, despite his brothers' evil intentions, God would work it all out in the end.

When everything around us screams the opposite of what God planted in our hearts, it can be tempting to take those dreams and throw them away or question our own sanity for believing in them. But maybe, like with Joseph, those dreams are a special grace. Maybe they are a declaration of God's faithfulness before we see it with our eyes. Maybe it's God's

DAY 12: REMAIN FAITHFUL

way of saying, "I'm telling you this now so that when things get rough and this dream looks impossible, you can be assured that I will be faithful to deliver on it."

Flip to John 14:15-31 and read it. How does this passage relate to Joseph's story?

This passage in John comes toward the end of Jesus' ministry on earth. He is hours away from going to the cross, but He's using those last moments to leave His disciples with a few words of promise. Along with all of these words about the coming of the Holy Spirit and the work Jesus is about to accomplish on the cross, He makes a statement.

Write down Jesus' words from verse 29.

Sometimes God gives us a heads-up about what's coming, not to be cruel to us in the waiting season, but so that when His word finally does come about, our faith can grow.

God was faithful with the dream He planted in Joseph's heart. We can trust Him to be faithful with us too.

Is there a dream in your heart that you believe God has planted?

IN THE WAITING

How can you remain faithful to God while you wait for that dream to come about?

Day 13: God is Still Working in the Silence

Enslaved Israel

EXODUS 1, MALACHI 3-4

IN THE WAITING

Today's reading in Malachi marks the end of the Old Testament. With just the flip of a page or two we're in the New Testament and Jesus' genealogy is announcing the fulfillment of the promised Messiah in Matthew 1. But did you know 400 years passed between the end of Malachi and the beginning of the Gospel of Matthew? During those 400 years, the only thing the people heard from God was silence. He didn't speak through prophets. He didn't appear in visions. He was quiet. Silent. For generations.

That period of 400 years reminds me of the years Israel spent enslaved to Egypt. Israel had ended up in Egypt because of a famine that overtook the land shortly after Joseph was raised up to second in command over Egypt. Behind the scenes, God had moved Joseph into a position of power that allowed him not only to provide food for the Egyptians, but also for his family in Canaan. Eventually, Joseph moves his father, brothers and their families to Egypt. Time passed, Joseph died, and a new Pharaoh rose to power who knew nothing about the Hebrew who had once helped guide Egypt into prosperity. Feeling threatened by the growing population of the Hebrew people, Pharaoh enslaved them. For hundreds of years the people cried out to God and begged for Him to deliver them.

As far as we know, God didn't speak during that time either. Generations were born and died still enslaved, probably wondering if the God of their fathers Abraham, Isaac, and Jacob was actually listening; and if He was listening, why wasn't He doing anything about the fact that they were slaves?

We, like Israel, can fall into this belief that God's silence means that He is absent, but that just isn't true. Just because God is quiet, it does not mean He isn't present and isn't working.

Read Exodus 2. In what ways do you see God working, even though He isn't speaking?

We also see this truth in the Gospels. Though the Bible doesn't record anything about the years of silence between the Old and New Testaments, we see God's hand at work as John the Baptist is born, fulfilling Malachi's prophecy and preparing the way for Messiah. We see Jesus, born of a virgin and fulfilling so many Old Testament prophecies.

God's silence also did not make His previous words irrelevant. Israel—the generations in Egypt, and the generations that lived during the silent years between Testaments—had God's words to cling to. Though He wasn't saying anything new, they had His Word written down and taught to them. These words were part of their daily lives and they repeated

DAY 13: GOD IS STILL WORKING IN THE SILENCE

them often. They clung to the words God had spoken previously until they heard Him speak something new.

If God feels silent right now in your own story, remember that His silence doesn't mean He's abandoned you. His silence does not mean He has stopped working in your life. His silence simply means it's time to lean in a little closer, wait a little longer, and trust that God is still working, even if you can't hear Him, and even if you don't see that work right now.

Is God silent right now? If so, how do you feel about that?

What words of encouragement, comfort, or promise has God spoken to you previously that you can continue to cling to until you hear from Him again?

How does Israel's story of waiting encourage you in yours?

Day 14: One More Minute

Israel at the Red Sea

EXODUS 13:17-14:31

IN THE WAITING

One of the perks of attending a Christian university was that many of my professors began their classes with a short devotion and prayer. One of the best devotions I've ever heard came mid semester during my Personal Evangelism class. I still remember it because it came at a point when I was knee-deep in a hard season of waiting and I was just about ready to give up.

My professor took us to this passage in Exodus where Israel's prayer for deliverance had been answered. They've left Egypt and are headed to the Promised Land; except now, there's a pretty big problem: Pharaoh's chariots are hot on their heels and they are trapped between the oncoming army and the Red Sea. For obvious reasons the Israelites start freaking out. It seems they've come out of Egypt only to die in the wilderness shortly after finding freedom.

Before we go further with that Red Sea situation, let's back up to the beginning of today's passage because there's something there in those final verses of chapter 13 that always gets me.

Look at Exodus 13:17-18. When God leads Israel out of Egypt, there are two directions He could lead them—the direct way through Philistine territory or the less direct route through the wilderness.

Which route does God choose and what reasoning does He give?

I look at that bit of insight and my heart softens toward this God who didn't want the Israelites to feel defeated before their freedom even began. The Red Sea might look like an impossible obstacle, but God knows it's the less intimidating one and He's already got a plan. Israel, however, doesn't know that. They don't know what the long way to the sea was saving them from. And even though they had seen God's power in delivering them out of Egypt, they don't yet see His ability to save them from Pharaoh's pursuing army on the banks of the Red Sea.

God has a plan here, and He's thought it through much more than the people believe. Moses knows, though. He knows God wouldn't lead them this far only to abandon them to death and defeat, so he speaks up.

DAY 14: ONE MORE MINUTE

What assurance does Moses give to Israel in Exodus 14:13-14?

In this impossible place, Moses assures Israel of God's deliverance if they just stay put and be quiet. No freaking out. No running away. No trying to make a way on their own. Just be still and expect God to move.

My professor when he shared this devotion with our Evangelism class, phrased it this way: "When you feel like you can't wait one more minute, wait one more minute."

There's this funny pattern I notice in other people's stories of waiting. Just past the point where they want to give up is when God moves. It's almost like God is saying, "Are you going to trust me to come through for you, even if it seems like I'm leading you the long way or showing up at the last minute?"

Israel was commanded to wait, stand firm, and see God's deliverance. And you know what? It happened. God came through. The Lord put a column of fire between Israel and Pharaoh's oncoming army to guard the people throughout the night. He blew back the sea and led the people across on dry land and into freedom. When Pharaoh's army tried to follow, they were swallowed up by the sea.

God delivered them, not just out of Egypt and slavery, but also from the pursuing army. He led them into freedom just as He promised. He led them into something new—something they'd prayed for generations to receive. They just didn't get there through the route they expected, and they almost missed it because they were ready to run in fear, rather than wait for the miracle.

We all have our ideas of how our waiting should play out. We have the roadmap and timelines all planned, but when things take longer or obstacles arise, we may face that same desire to flee that Israel felt. We may give into the idea that God has only led us this far to abandon us right here in the worst possible spot. Maybe your situation isn't as dire, but perhaps your heart is tired of waiting. You're tired of investing in faith when you're not even sure God is going to come through. Maybe you have reached the point where you're not sure you can wait another minute. If that is your situation, I encourage you wait one more minute. Don't quit yet. Perhaps God's deliverance is just around the corner. You never know what kinds of things God kept you from, what ways He provided for you and protected you by leading you this way. Things turned out pretty well for Israel, and I believe that even if your wait doesn't end the way you want it to, God's got this handled. You can trust Him to come through.

Describe a time in the past where you have felt like giving up on God for something? Did you give up, or did you wait around and see Him come through?

Looking at your waiting now, do you feel like God's been leading you the long way? How might the long way actually be the best way?

How does Israel's deliverance at the Red Sea encourage you in your own waiting?

Day 15: Remember God's Presence

Israel at Sinai

EXODUS 32:1-35

IN THE WAITING

During their exodus from Egypt, Israel saw some pretty amazing stuff. After 400 years of silence, God finally moved. He called a man named Moses to lead Israel out of Egypt. God revealed His power, might, and justice to the Egyptians through the ten plagues. After Passover, God led Israel out into the wilderness, headed in the direction of the land God had promised to Abraham and his descendants. Along the way, Israel thought they were goners when Pharaoh's army pursued them, but once again, God showed His power, divided the Red Sea, and led Israel safely through on dry ground. On the other side of the sea, He led the people, displaying His presence in the form of a pillar of cloud and fire, and settled them at the base of Mount Sinai.

It's at this mountain that God begins to establish Israel as their own nation, with Him as their ruler. He calls Moses up the mountain to receive the Law and the people wait eagerly for Moses to return.

And they wait.

And they wait.

And they wait.

After 40 days, when Moses still hasn't come back, the people begin to think that he has died up there on the mountain in God's presence. So the people go to Aaron, Moses' brother, and demand, "Come, make gods for us who will go before us because Moses, the man who brought us up from the land of Egypt, we don't know what happened to him!" (verse 1)

It seems like a silly demand for the people to make. After all, they just experienced God's goodness in leading them out of Egypt. They saw His signs and miracles and wonders. Just a few chapters before, on Moses' first trip up the mountain, God delivers the Ten Commandments with very clear instruction about idol worship.

Read Exodus 20:1-6. What is God's command about idol worship?

Israel has encountered God in so many ways, and while Moses is away receiving further instruction about worship and the Tabernacle, the people have heard what God requires. He is to be their only God. Idol worship is strictly forbidden. My rule-following brain wants to

DAY 15: REMEMBER GOD'S PRESENCE

scream at the Israelites on the page because it's just so clear: a golden idol is not a great idea.

But if I can infuse a little grace here, let's remember that Israel spent 400 years living in a nation where temples were set up to honor the many Egyptian gods. Each god had a physical representation that the people could look to in their worship. For Israel, I think Moses kind of filled that role. The people didn't worship Moses, but they definitely relied on him to reveal God to them and speak the words God gave him. The people of Israel are still young in their faith and dependence on God. He's delivered them, yes, but they don't know how to do life with Him yet—they don't know how to trust Him—and since Moses seems to have vanished, they need something physical to cling to.

While there is grace to understand their mindset in making such a demand, that doesn't mean it was a good idea. When Aaron melts down the peoples' jewelry and casts an image of a golden calf, then declares it as Israel's god, the Lord's anger burns against Israel. Moses heads back down the mountain to see what the issue is and finds Israel dancing around the golden calf. What ensues next is pretty intense. Moses confronts his brother and people die that day for their sin. They got distracted and desperate, and they suffered the consequences for their choices.

In seasons of waiting we need to be on our guard. It's easy to look at Israel and declare that their actions are stupid. How could they do such a thing? But we are just as human as they are and in our own waiting stories it is just as easy for us to turn from God, to decide that we've waited long enough, to declare that He's not going to show, and set up our own idols. We may not melt down our valuables and watch a golden calf jump out of the fire, but we do other things. We throw ourselves into our work, hoping to make our own way. We manipulate and scheme and do what we think is best without seeking God's guidance and direction. Like with what Israel experienced at the Red Sea, when we quit early and go our own way, our relationship with God suffers and often find ourselves waiting even longer.

At this point I think it's worth reminding ourselves why we're here, why we're studying people's stories on waiting. The goal here is to draw closer to God in the waiting. It isn't to *get* that thing we're waiting for; it's to *know* God better, right here in this season of wanting.

Israel wanted something safe and visible, but the reality was that God had settled Himself at the peak of Sinai in the form of cloud and fire. He was very obviously present, but the people couldn't see it. They were too stuck in what they thought they needed and it drove a wedge between them and God. Instead of drawing near, they pushed Him away.

I know the ache of waiting. I know how easy it is to allow our attention to rest on that thing we want, but friend, let's not forget God in all of this. Let's not miss out on the very obvious ways He is present. Nothing we're waiting for will ever satisfy us like relationship with God. God may use our wants to draw us near, but He also uses the waiting. Don't let your heart settle for less than God. Ask Him to show you where He is present right here in this season. Ask Him to increase your desire for Him, more than the thing you want.

IN THE WAITING

In what ways is God revealing His presence to you right here and now?

Have you been settling for less than God? Confess that to God and ask Him to increase your desire for Him.

In what ways might you be prioritizing the thing you have been waiting for, over waiting for God Himself?

Day 16: When the Waiting Isn't Your Fault

Caleb

NUMBERS 13:1-14:25

In today's passage we pick up with Israel's story as they stand on the brink of seeing God's covenant to Abraham fulfilled. They can almost taste the milk and honey. In preparation for entering the land, twelve spies are sent into the land to see what it is they are walking into—to see if it really is everything God has promised and what kind of obstacles they will be facing when they enter the land. When the spies return, they affirm the beauty and prosperity of the land. The people of the land, however, pose a threat. They are huge and numerous, and they have ten of the twelve spies shaking in their sandals. These ten spies are adamant that if they walk into that land to take it, Israel will be completely crushed.

Caleb is adamant too, except he's on the opposite side of the argument. What is Caleb's perspective about the land and what Israel should do?

Caleb is convinced that taking this new land isn't about Israel's ability; it's all about God's faithfulness. If He promised, He will deliver. But the people can't see that. All they see are the obstacles. They are leaning on their own understanding rather than resting in the faithfulness of the same God who brought them out of Egypt and got them through the Red Sea on dry ground.

Israel's unbelief costs them the Promised Land. Because they rejected God's promise and do not believe His goodness in helping them take the land, their generation will die in the wilderness and they will not live in the land He had promised.

Caleb and Joshua, the only two who believed that God would lead them safely into the land of abundance, will be the only ones from their generation to go. Unfortunately their entry into the Promised Land is delayed 40 years because of the people's lack of trust.

The waiting caused by the actions or decisions of others can be especially hard. This kind of waiting can be a breeding ground for bitterness toward those that stuck us in the waiting. Bitterness toward God can also grow. It doesn't seem fair. Why should we be punished because of someone else's choices?

Here's the hard and beautiful truth about how God has established this world and how sin taints it. When God created the world, there were two gifts He gave us: The gift of community (the whole "it is not good for man to be alone" thing doesn't just apply to marriage relationships), and the gift of free will.

DAY 16: WHEN THE WAITING ISN'T YOUR FAULT

Read Genesis 2:4-17. In what way is the gift of free will presented in the Garden?

There have been times I've wondered why God would stick both the Tree of Knowledge of Good and Evil in the Garden. Why plant both of them? With the planting of those two trees God gave us choice. He has been a relational God from the very beginning. He will not force Himself on us. Rather, He invites us to choose Him.

Israel had the choice to trust God and enter the Promised Land, or trust themselves and lean on their own understanding. They chose the latter. That decision affected the entire community, including the two who were ready to faithfully trust God's promises.

So how do we handle the waiting when it isn't our fault? How do we wait well and draw near to God in the process when our waiting is the result of other people's choices?

I think it begins with honest conversation with God. I think it begins with telling Him how we feel during every leg of the waiting. I think it means being vigilant to not let bitterness take root, either toward God or the ones we blame for our wait. It also means learning how to extend grace and forgiveness, which is easier said than done.

I think it's also important to remember that God's plans stand firm no matter what. His promises remain true. Israel did eventually enter the Promised Land, Joshua and Caleb with them. The previous generation missed out, but the new one walked in, faithfully following the Lord.

I know it can feel like you've missed the boat, that somehow the choices of others have made that one thing completely impossible. But know this: God's plans stand firm. His words will come to pass. If there is something He has spoken to you, you can trust Him to deliver on it, even if it takes more time than you anticipated. The actions of others cannot eliminate God's plans for you.

Read Joshua 14:6-12. How does this event of Caleb finally entering the land encourage you in your own wait?

IN THE WAITING

Are you holding on to any bitterness toward God or someone else you blame for your waiting season? Don't go another day carrying around that unnecessary burden. Confess that here and ask God to heal your heart.

Day 17: The Hope and Grief of Waiting

Rahab

JOSHUA 2:1-24; 6:22-25

IN THE WAITING

Rahab is one of those people in Scripture that I wish we had more backstory on. With the exception of Hagar, the Egyptian maidservant of Sarah, every other person we've talked about so far has been part of Abraham's family. Rahab is not. At least not initially. She resides in the city of Jericho, the first stop of Israel's conquest after 40 years of desert wandering. And to make matters more interesting, Rahab is a prostitute.

Rahab's introduction is humorous to me. Before we meet her, Joshua sends out two spies to go into Jericho and scope it out. Not even a verse later, we find the spies lodging in the house of a prostitute named Rahab. I laugh because we have no idea how they came to be there, we just know that's where they ended up. I imagine Rahab standing on a corner, a normal part of her routine, when she notices men who look foreign, but are obviously trying to blend in. Perhaps she uses some of her learned charms to get some information out of them, or maybe something in her gut tells her these are men she needs to become allies with. However it happened, Rahab's words to the spies reveal that this meeting is a divine appointment. Despite her occupation and her place of residence, Rahab is a woman of faith.

Stories of Israel's God have traveled from Egypt, and she has heard all about how the God of Israel conquered Egypt and parted the sea and led His people to freedom. She's heard about the Israelite's victory over the Amorite kings and the power displayed by their God, and she believes. Rahab believes enough to make a statement of faith, but she also backs up her belief with action.

What does Rahab say and do that proves her faith in God?

Rahab helps the men escape through her window, conveniently located in the outer wall of the city, and ties a scarlet chord in her window as a testimony of her faithfulness in not ratting them out. That chord also serves as a reminder of the spies' promise to spare her and her family when Israel comes to conquer her city.

That day, a high-stakes kind of waiting began for Rahab. Her life and the lives of her family depended on the spies keeping their promise. As the days passed and the scarlet chord remained dangling outside her window, I'm sure Rahab began to battle questions: Would the spies keep their promise? Would their God even accept her? With her city about to be destroyed, did she dare dream about what her new life would be like?

DAY 17: THE HOPE AND GRIEF OF WAITING

Waiting can stir up a lot of complicated emotions.

As much as I wish we knew more about Rahab's past, I'm certain it's not much of a stretch to imagine her beginning to dream about her new life outside of Jericho. Maybe prostitution wasn't a life she'd chosen for herself. Maybe she was forced into it or driven to it as the only way to provide for herself. Maybe up until the encounter with the spies, she'd had no choice about what her future looked like. Now she did. And she chose to take action in hiding the Israelite spies and then waiting for their return. She chose to believe the stories she'd heard about God. She chose faith and she chose risk. All in the hope of receiving a new life, a better life—the life of one grafted into God's family.

With all of that hope, though, I imagine Rahab was also feeling a lot of grief. The reality of this particular waiting is tied with the harsh reality that, while Rahab and her family will be saved, her city was about to be destroyed. Her people were about to be slaughtered and the land taken over. That's a lot of emotion to carry—hope of something completely new and the grief over what is about to be lost.

Maybe what you're feeling in the waiting is complicated. You want that new thing, but you also feel the weight of grief in your situation too. Perhaps the situation isn't as dire as Rahab's, but your heart feels heavy. You yearn for a drastic change. Can I encourage you and tell you that it's okay—and necessary, even—to sit with both of those things? You can hold hope and you can hold grief together. It's complicated and messy and it feels heavy, but I think that's part of the waiting—sitting in the mess and the unknowns.

Rahab is an excellent example of this. She had hope for a new beginning for her and her family, but I believe she also grieved for her city. A fresh start was coming, but she needed space to hold grief and hope together. She did that by choosing to hold onto faith.

What kind of fresh start does your heart need? Take time to talk with the Lord about it and ask Him to show you what one thing you can do today to step into that fresh start.

IN THE WAITING

How have you felt that kind of weight of complicated emotions in your waiting? How have you experienced the weight of carrying hope for something new along with grief?

Day 18: Be Assured

Gideon

JUDGES 6:1-24, 33-40

IN THE WAITING

Waiting can begin for so many different reasons and in so many different ways. We've seen that throughout the stories we've studied. Some waiting is initiated by God. Some waiting stems from desire. Some waiting is caused by the decisions and actions of others. But there is another kind of waiting we've yet to explore, one we find in Gideon's story. This is the kind of waiting that begins when we feel a nudge to something new, something more, but we're not quite sure what to do about it. We think we've heard from God, but we feel unsure, so we enter into this season of active waiting, testing to see if that call we feel really is from God.

Gideon's personal call came in a time of communal waiting. When we meet him, Gideon is threshing wheat in a wine press. He's not there because he doesn't know the proper way to take care of the wheat that's been harvested. He's hiding out with his wheat in a wine press because Israel has been taken over by the Midianites and this foreign nation has been taking all of Israel's food. Circumstances in Israel are pretty dire, and the people are waiting for relief.

It's at that point that an angel of the Lord pays Gideon a visit and delivers a message: "Go in the strength you have and deliver Israel form the grasp of Midian. I am sending you!" (verse 14)

I love that "Go in the strength that you have" part. God doesn't call Gideon to go to boot camp or start a training program. Instead He calls Gideon to make use of what he already has and assures Gideon that God is backing him up. God is calling Gideon to be part of the solution, part of His plan to rescue Israel from Midian's oppression, but Gideon is wary.

What makes Gideon doubt God's call?

On top of the fact that this man is hiding from the enemy, Gideon's pedigree isn't impressive. Of all the men God could have chosen to lead an attack against Midian, Gideon feels the least qualified. He's the youngest of his family. His family is weak and part of one of the smaller tribes in Israel. Surely, there is someone else better qualified for such a task.

Gideon is also concerned about God's presence. Though the angel greets him with a friendly, "The Lord is with you, valiant warrior," Gideon can't help but question God's presence.

DAY 18: BE ASSURED

Look again at verse 13. What makes Gideon doubt God's presence?

So, Gideon has a call—to deliver Israel from Midian's oppression—but he also has doubts.

I can relate. There have been times God has laid things on my heart or put an opportunity in front of me or invited me to something new, and I hesitated. I wanted to know that things would work out. But I think what God wants us to understand instead is that, no matter the outcome, He's with us. He is always present.

That is something Gideon needed to understand. For seven years Israel has lived under the oppression of the Midianites. In some ways it probably seemed like God had abandoned Israel. Gideon wanted to be assured of God's presence.

I think that's why God was so patient with Gideon's fleece test. Things might have been different if, when the angel approached Gideon and gave him the mission, Gideon had tightened his belt and set off to deliver Israel in his own strength. Instead, Gideon acknowledged his weakness and wasn't willing to move forward without some assurance that, despite how circumstances seemed, God hadn't abandoned Israel. Gideon wanted to make sure that if he moved forward, God would be with Him.

Instead of running away or rushing ahead, Gideon waits. He asks God for confirmation that Gideon truly is the one God is calling to this task. He needs a physical, tangible sign. So he throws out a fleece and asks God to make the fleece wet and the ground dry. When God answers, Gideon asks a second time, this time for the fleece to be dry and the ground wet.

As soon as Gideon got that second fleece answer, he jumps into action and works with God the whole way through. Even when God strips down his army to almost nothing, Gideon faithfully obeys because he knows the God he is following. He is assured of God's presence, and Gideon knows what his role is. His short season of waiting provided time for his heart settle in on what God was calling him to and to put his trust in what God had promised.

Not all waiting seasons we find ourselves in are long-winded. Some are short and sweet and full of intention. Sometimes we wait because we aren't sure of our next step. If you're waiting for God to confirm a call, don't use waiting as a way to stall. Gideon's story shows us that God is willing to honor our need to wait a little bit for some confirmation on what we feel called to, but once we get our answer, we need to be ready to move like Gideon. Don't prolong the wait, even if what God is calling you to feels scary and overwhelming. He is with you. You will not move forward alone.

IN THE WAITING

What answers or affirmations are you seeking God for right now in your waiting?

Is there something God has asked you to take action on, but you haven't done anything yet? Name the thing and ask God how to move forward. If you already know what to do, make a commitment today to take that next step.

Day 19: Allowed to Want

Hannah

1 SAMUEL 1:1-18

Hannah is not the first woman we've studied who wants a child. Sarah and Rachel both faced a similar wait, but their stories unfolded differently. While the objects of our wait might be the same, our stories are all different. Where Sarah took matters into her own hands and Rachel competed, Hannah sought the Lord.

What tugs at my heart so strongly about Hannah's story is that it explores this idea of wanting. I think too often we're taught that wanting is wrong or a sign that we're not content in the Lord. We read passages like Psalm 23:1 where David writes, "The Lord is my Shepherd, I shall not want," or hear sermons about contentment and begin to feel guilty or even shamed for wanting something. There is a kind of wanting that causes harm—the kind of wanting that is marked by getting more or being better than the other person or filling our lives with stuff. But there is another kind of wanting, a holy wanting that says, "What I have is good, but there is more. There is a deep desire in my heart that I want God to fulfill." That's the kind of wanting Hannah experiences.

Hannah is the favorite wife of her husband, and he dotes on her. Though she is childless, some would call her blessed because she has the love of her husband. We know the ache of the woman who lacked that kind of love in Leah's story. Hannah's husband tried to ease her pain of wanting by reminding her of what she did have. "Am I not better than ten sons?" he asked her (verse 8). While Hannah had the love of her husband, we all know that when we want something else so desperately, asking us to be content with what we have can make matters worse.

Contentment does not mean we don't have wants.

Hannah wants a son desperately, so much so that the rival wife's abuse finally gets the better of Hannah during a feast in Shiloh. Looking for relief, she runs straight to the tabernacle and falls face down before the Lord.

I love that this is Hannah's response. It's not to go slap Penninah—though, Lord knows that probably would have been my response. She doesn't demand that her husband sleep with her because maybe this time she'll be able to conceive. Hannah doesn't take matters into her own hands to get what she so desperately wants. Instead, she lays her desire before God, and that process is quite messy. She is weeping and sobbing and praying so intensely that her lips are moving but no words are coming out. The priest mistakes her heart-pouring prayer as drunkenness and calls her out on it.

Has your wanting ever manifested itself in a way that brought correction from others? How did you respond in that situation?

DAY 19: ALLOWED TO WAIT

Hannah assures Eli that she is not drunk, but praying out of the depth of her pain. Her prayer reminds me that even when I want something to the point of feeling broken and I've reached the point of desperation in my wanting, I can bring that before God.

God doesn't condemn us for wanting. In fact, He invites us to lay it all bear and broken before Him. Every want. Every desire. Every desperate plea. Every bit of brokenness and resentment and anguish—He welcomes it all.

Sometimes in the waiting I wonder if I'm still waiting because I want the wrong thing or I want that one thing too much. I wonder if waiting is God's way of correcting me, a way for Him to realign my desires. Maybe at times the waiting is about Him giving us new desires, like He did with Rahab, but Hannah's story assures me I can come broken and battered and bruised. I can be painfully honest with God about the pain of waiting and ask for Him to come through. No matter how things turn out in the end, God welcomes us with open arms. He invites us to climb up onto His lap or fall on our knees or lay prostrate before Him and just be honest.

We are allowed to want, and sometimes when we let ourselves sit in that honest, wanting place, we actually find blessing.

What blessing did Eli speak over Hannah before sending her off?

I want to send you off in peace today, dear heart. I want you to know that whatever desires you carry in your heart matter to God. Part of being content is embracing the place you are at with joy, but that doesn't nullify your desire for something more.

We can carry desire and we can carry contentment at the same time.

We've talked about a lot of people who did not wait well, and we've been challenged by their stories of what not to do. Today, I want to encourage you to be like Hannah. Bring your honest heart before the Lord and allow the depth of your longing to be a point of connection with Him.

IN THE WAITING

Have you been completely honest with the Lord about what you're waiting for? Have you told Him how you feel about your waiting? Get honest with God today. Tell Him what you want. Tell Him how you feel about all this waiting. And then go in peace.

Day 20: Revived Hope

Ruth

RUTH 1-3

IN THE WAITING

Some seasons of waiting that challenge our ability to keep hoping, while other seasons reignite our hope. That's the kind of waiting Ruth finds herself in after leaving Boaz in the field.

When Ruth and Naomi returned from Moab, both women were widows, and the life they'd planned for themselves had died with their husbands. While Naomi's heart sank into bitterness, Ruth gave her heart over to love. She committed herself to Naomi even when it meant leaving home and the hopes of marrying again to journey to a new land where she wasn't welcome. Ruth joyfully accepted her new life because of her love for Naomi, even when it meant poverty and collecting leftovers in someone else's field.

Ruth's care and attention began to heal Naomi's heart, and as Naomi softened, her eyes were opened once again to God's hand in their lives. After all, who but God could orchestrate these events? There are too many "just so happened" things happening here. Ruth just so happens to find a field of Naomi's relative to glean in. This man, Boaz, just so happens to be one of two men who could redeem these two women and provide for them. It all looks like more than just coincidence to Naomi. This is providence and Naomi decides to take advantage of it. She hatches a scheme and sends Ruth to the place she knows Boaz will be.

What does Naomi ask Ruth to do?

Still taking care of her mother-in-law, Ruth does what is necessary, asking Boaz to be her kinsman redeemer and essentially proposing to him. Despite the vulnerability she must have felt in such a situation, I think this whole scene in the field reawakens hope for Ruth too. She had lovingly and joyfully given up her life and committed her future to serve the God of Israel and to serve Naomi. In the process, she had laid aside the dreams that were no doubt hidden in her heart. She gave up waiting on something that may or may not come in the future—after all, who would marry a Moabite?

But God has a funny, gracious way of reviving those deceased hopes, and blessing us in ways we never thought we'd experience.

While Ruth's wait was short, because Boaz dealt with the other man and made plans to marry Ruth that same day, it awakened hope in her. Her faithfulness in living in the moment, in loving Naomi well was rewarded, and in her marriage to Boaz, Ruth became part of the direct line of Jesus and the great-grandmother of King David.

DAY 20: REVIVED HOPE

Maybe this is the kind of waiting you're experiencing—a season of renewing your hope. You've poured yourself into the people and opportunities right in front of you, even giving up some of your own dreams in the process, and now God has you waiting as He revives those dreams. This is a beautiful season. Embrace it. It may not be easy to wait, and it might even feel painful to have those old hopes resurrected, but allow God to revive the broken and forgotten places of your heart. Allow Him to revive your hope and find joy in the coming unexpected blessings.

What hopes have you let die that maybe God wants to revive?

What encouragement do you find in Ruth's waiting?

Day 21: Part of a Bigger Story

David

2 SAMUEL 7

IN THE WAITING

David knows about waiting. For years before he took the throne as Israel's king, he spent his life on the run. The prophet Samuel had anointed David as a teenager way back in 1 Samuel 6, and while David waited for God to fulfill his calling, he spent much of his time trying not to die at Saul's hand. Saul, the first king of Israel, was a jealous king who lost sight of what mattered and forgot the God who gave him his position. After Saul dies in battle, God keeps His promise and puts David, the former shepherd boy, on the throne.

In the first few verses of today's reading, we see the long struggle of waiting finally put to an end. David has settled into his position. His enemies have been dealt with, and as he looks around at the grandeur of his palace, he remembers God. He remembers the Ark of the Covenant, the physical reminder of God's presence among His people, and David decides that he wants to build a more permanent place for the ark and God's presence to dwell. When David expresses this desire, Nathan encourages the king to set to work on building this temple, assuring him that God is with David. Yet in the very next verse, God delivers a message to Nathan for David.

At first it almost feels like Nathan spoke out of turn when he told David to start building, but the further I read in this passage, the more I begin to wonder if maybe David's desire is God-planted.

The day David shares his desire to build God a permanent dwelling is the day God makes some incredible declarations about Israel and about David's family line. God establishes a covenant with David and promises to make David's family great. Sounds a little like God's covenant with Abraham. Beyond David's desire to build a place of worship, God is continuing to build a greater story.

Read Matthew 1:1-17. What bigger story do you see unfolding here?

As we dig deeper into God's story and these stories of waiting, I am beginning to see how so much of everyone's waiting ties back to that covenant God made with Abraham.

DAY 21: PART OF A BIGGER STORY

Starting with Abraham, list all of the big picture ideas and stories we've talked about so far. How do they connect to the covenant with Abraham?

Remember back in our Bible study skills section how I mentioned that understanding the big picture of the story of Scripture was one of those skills we'd be building in this study? Though all of these stories are about individuals, they tell the greater story of God. Every time we encounter a new story, we connect it to what we've already studied.

How do you see the greater story of God woven through the first half of study?

As with many prophecies, God's response to David has both present and future ramifications. In just a few years, God's word is fulfilled through David's son Solomon. David himself will not build God's temple, but his son will, and Israel will experience one of its wealthiest, most peaceful points in history under Solomon's reign. But God's word about building a house through David also points to Jesus, who several generations later, would become the new focal point, the new center of God's presence among His people.

So while David's wait to be king is over, he enters into a new season of waiting—waiting to see God's covenant come to fruition. David wants to build the temple, but God asks David to prepare the way for his son Solomon to do the work, and he does so faithfully.

David got to see and experience the fulfillment of God's promise that David would be king of Israel. However, he won't see the fulfillment of this new promise—of the temple or the ultimate fulfillment through Jesus. But like Noah, David does the work he is given to do. He provides Solomon with everything he needs to build the temple, and he trusts God with the rest.

This is the bittersweet side of waiting. We never know how long our waiting will last, and sometimes that thing we're waiting for isn't actually for us to see. Sometimes the work we're called to do in the waiting prepares the way for someone else to see the fruit. Even then, let's be faithful in the waiting. Let's trust God to do what He's promised, even if we never get to see it.

How do you feel about the idea that some waiting involves preparing the way for someone else? Are you willing to still do the work even if you never get to enjoy the fruit?

How does David's story encourage you in your waiting?

Day 22: The Loneliness of Waiting

Elijah

1 KINGS 18:20-19:18

There is a lot going on in this story. When we jump into Elijah's ministry in 1 Kings 18, Israel is in the midst of a famine that has been going on for three years. The famine was a consequence for Israel's unfaithfulness, Ahab's poor leadership, and his wife's idolatry. In an effort to draw Israel back to the one true God, Elijah and Ahab meet for a showdown of the gods to determine who the true God is. Two alters are built and an ox placed on each alter—one alter for Baal and one for Yahweh. The worshipers of Baal call out to their god, and Elijah calls out to Yahweh, and whichever god sends down fire is the true god.

The worshipers of Baal call out for hours with no heavenly reply, but when Elijah humbles himself in prayer, asking God to show Himself so that the people's hearts would return to Him, God answers with fire, and the ox, the wood, the stones, and even the dirt around the alter are all burnt up. Baal's worshipers are killed, and Elijah prays for rain to once again fall on the land.

After such a dramatic display of God's presence and power, you'd think Elijah would be celebrating in victory. Instead, he's on the run for his life because when Jezebel learned about what Elijah had done to her priests, she promised to do the same to Elijah and end his life. Elijah then flees to the wilderness. As he falls exhausted under a tree, he asks God for death. He has flat out hit his limit with this whole prophet gig. He's done and believes only death will bring him relief.

Instead of death, Elijah falls into a deep sleep and is awakened by an angel who provides two meals for Elijah between naps, giving him strength for the 40 day trek into the wilderness to Mount Horeb.

Fun fact: Mount Horeb is the same place Moses met God in the burning bush. It's the same place where Moses received the call to go back to Pharaoh and demand Israel's freedom. It is also the place where Israel camps out for a year after being rescued from Egypt, and the place where God gives this new nation the Law.

Horeb is a location with a reputation for powerful encounters with God. Perhaps that's why Elijah ends up in a cave in that mountain.

While at Horeb, the Lord comes to Elijah and asks, "What are you doing here, Elijah?" Elijah replies that he is the only faithful one left in Israel.

This response is one Elijah has given throughout this passage. Skim back through today's reading and find all the instances where Elijah makes the claim that he is the only one left faithful to God and write them down.

DAY 22: THE LONELINESS OF WAITING

Elijah feels alone. He's looking around and all he sees is how everyone else has abandoned the Lord, and he alone has remained faithful. While it might seem this way from Elijah's perspective, it isn't true.

Earlier in chapter 18 we learn about a man named Obadiah who worked for Ahab. When the famine began and Jezebel started killing God's prophets, Obadiah gathered up one hundred prophets and hid them in a cave. Elijah is aware of this because Obadiah told him about it (18:2-15), but that was three years ago. Even if the prophets are still alive in that cave, that doesn't negate the fact that right here on Mount Horeb, with Jezebel seeking to kill him, Elijah feels utterly alone.

He admits that to God, and then God calls Elijah to stand in His presence.

How does God reveal His presence to Elijah and what information does He give the prophet?

In seasons of waiting, it can be easy to feel alone and abandoned. Perhaps you're waiting to enter that next phase of life and it seems like everyone else is moving ahead without you. Or maybe you've been praying and praying and, like Elijah, you've been faithful, but God hasn't seemed to keep His end of the bargain. You feel like He hasn't done His job and even He has abandoned you.

You know what I love about Elijah's story, though? I love that God provides for Elijah throughout his journey into the wilderness so that God can meet Elijah in his desperation. I love that God invites Elijah out of the safety of the dark cave and reveals Himself through a quiet whisper in the midst of so much upheaval. And I love that after God assures Elijah of His presence, He also gives Elijah the community partners he needs to keep doing the work God has called him to.

Friend, waiting is hard and lonely. There will be times when you don't want to admit it and you keep pushing forward because loneliness is a heavy emotion to carry. There will also be times, though, when it all feels like too much and you feel alone and you are in desperate need of a fresh encounter with God—when you need to be assured of His presence and that you aren't really alone. When those times come, or if you're in one right now, take the space you need and cry out to God. Get away, retreat, and ask God to meet with you, to reveal His ever-present presence to you. It's okay to ask for community too, for a few fellow wanderers to accompany you on your journey and help you keep going when you want to give up on all this waiting.

IN THE WAITING

How do you need to encounter God today?

Do you have a community of people you can lean on during this waiting season? If so, take a moment today to thank God for them. Maybe send your people a message thanking them for their presence in your life. If you don't have a community, ask God for a couple of people who can wait with you.

How does Elijah's story encourage you in your waiting?

Day 23: A Time of Preparation

Esther

ESTHER 2:15-4:17

IN THE WAITING

For such a time as this...

Mordecai's words must have echoed in Esther's mind as she remembered how she had come to be in the king's palace. Her road to the throne was one she never expected or wanted to take, yet here she is. She has power and position and now the heavy responsibility of standing up for her people and saving them from genocide. The request Mordecai made of her would cost her everything.

I imagine Esther felt her world tilt as the weight of it all settled over her. Her title as queen only carried so much power. If she went before the king unsummoned, she faced death, but Mordecai had been adamant that death was likely no matter her decision. If she went before the king, unless he granted her pardon and held out his scepter, she would die; but if she kept silent and let the edict be carried out, her people would perish and she with them.

What is Esther's response to Mordecai's request?

Esther could have said no. She could have refused to go before the king. She also could have hiked up her skirts and stomped right into the throne room that day. Instead, she asks for three days to prepare.

When Esther sends that response back to Mordecai, her waiting begins. The task ahead would take every ounce of her courage. Her request for Mordecai to gather some people and join her in fasting and praying for the next three days is meant as a time of preparation. Perhaps she is there for such a time as this, but if she was, she wants God's backing. She needs Him to go before her and deliver His people and her.

Sometimes in life we're faced with the waiting because the time is necessary to prepare us for what's ahead. Sometimes the things we're waiting on require training or entering into a certain mindset. Sometimes these things we want require courage, and courage isn't something you can muster up yourself. Fear can quickly squelch it if courage is placed in the wrong source. If we're going to step into this new thing we need to be secure in God. We need to believe that, no matter what happens, He's got us.

DAY 23: A TIME OF PREPARATION

Think of a time you needed to be courageous. Did you lean into God for courage or did you try to muster it up yourself? What was the outcome?

Esther set aside time to prepare. Stepping into something new, life changing—or in Esther's case, life-threatening—requires a certain amount of courage that can only be found in extended, intentional time with the Lord. Esther knew that. It's why she asked for three days. It's why she secluded herself and denied her body what it needed to sustain her because she needed the Lord to sustain her. It's why she asked Mordecai to gather the rest of their people, so that they could come together for the same purpose. She needed God and she needed the support and prayers of her community.

That's another beautiful part of Esther's story—her waiting was done in community. Physically, she was in the palace fasting with her handmaids, but in town her people gathered together to fast and pray with her. Despite how it must have felt three days later when Esther stepped into the throne room without invitation, she was not alone. She was surrounded and supported by a community who waited with her, and she was held up by the God she had spent her waiting days pressing into.

Trust the waiting period. Waiting can be a time of preparation, centering, grounding, and helping us place all of our hope and peace and purpose on Jesus.

In what ways do you notice this season of waiting being used as a time of preparation? Are there new skills you're developing, new relationships you're investing in, new ways you're connecting with God?

IN THE WAITING

Esther invited her community to wait with her in a specific way. How can you invite your community into the waiting with you?

Day 24: Stand Firm

Shadrack, Meeshack, and Abednego

DANIEL 3:1-19

This story has been a long-time favorite among Sunday school classes everywhere. It has all the great makings of a fantastic tale of honor and faithfulness—an evil king, three handsome heroes, and a dramatic rescue from a blazing furnace. Truly it's a story for the ages. But here's something we can sometimes forget about these Bible stories: the people who showed courage, claimed faith, and made scary choices did so without knowing how their story would end.

As Hebrew youth who were brought to live in exile in Babylon, Shadrack, Meshack, and Abednego proved themselves to be responsible and trustworthy. They were hard workers and showed great integrity. Because of their character, these three, along with Daniel, were promoted to be advisors to King Nebuchadnezzar. When the order came to bow before the king's enormous golden image, they refused, deciding instead to be faithful to their God.

While their choice is admirable, they made that choice knowing that one of two things would happen. Either God would come to their rescue or He would not and they would burn alive in the furnace.

They didn't know how things would play out, yet they chose to stand firm in their convictions. No matter what happened, they would remain faithful to their God.

The statement they make in verse 16-18 is powerful. What is your reaction to these words?

At some point in the waiting, we're faced with the same choice. While a crazy king may not threaten to throw us into fire, we reach a point where we have to decide if we're going to trust God and remain faithful to Him no matter the outcome. He may come through in the way we hope or He may not. We have to choose where our faith and hope land if we don't get what we want. It's a hard and painful thing to wrestle with, but it's worth wrestling down, even if it takes time. And frankly, it's probably a decision we'll have to wrestle with multiple times in our lives.

Is what you're waiting for worth sacrificing your relationship with God? Have you allowed that thing you're waiting for to be an idol? Maybe it's not gold and ninety feet tall, but if it's occupying space and demanding more of your attention and love than you're devoting to God, perhaps it's time to do some reevaluating. Will you choose to stand firm like Shadrack, Meeshack, and Abednego? Will you trust God no matter what happens? Will you remain faithful to Him even if His answer to your waiting is no?

DAY 24: STAND FIRM

God is the only constant, the only One who stays. That thing you're waiting for may not come to pass, or maybe it will, but eventually even that thing will run its course. The job ends, the child grows up and moves away, the spouse dies, the money runs out. That's not to put a damper on things or to convince you to stop wanting. It's just a reminder that the only permanent thing in this life is God, His love, and His grace. His presence remains even when everything else fades away.

Have you idolized the thing you're waiting for or placed more value on it than you have on God? Confess that now and ask God to re-center your affections and attention on Him.

In what way does today's study encourage or challenge you in your own wait?

Day 25: Check Your Attitude

Jonah

JONAH 1-4

Jonah's wait is an odd one. Just about every other person we're studying is waiting on something that we would call good, whether that be a child, release, rescue, freedom, or for God to come through on His promises. But at the end of the book of Jonah, we find this prophet waiting for God to destroy a group of people Jonah believes is beyond redemption.

Have you ever experienced a Jonah-style waiting where you've wanted something bad to happen to someone else?

When we meet Jonah in his twisted sort of waiting, the sun is sweltering and the wind is harsh as Jonah sits on his perch above the city of Nineveh. Yet, the weather seems an appropriate companion to the scorching emotions ravaging his heart. It's easy to picture Jonah with arms crossed tightly, eyes locked on the city, grumbling to himself. "I knew this would happen; I just knew it. God gives me words of repentance for the Ninevites and the whole city has instituted a fast. These people don't deserve God's mercy."

Even from this distance, Jonah hears the wailing as the people turn to the Lord. Of course the Lord shows mercy. That's why God called Jonah to Nineveh in the first place. It doesn't matter a person's nationality or their past or what sins they have committed; if they were sincere, God will forgive them.

God shows mercy on the repentant people of Nineveh, just as He promised—just as Jonah knew God would. In fact, God's mercy and grace are the very reason Jonah ran in the opposite direction in the first place. He didn't want to see Nineveh forgiven; he wanted to see them demolished by fire from heaven.

Maybe it was Jonah's pride in his own self-righteousness that made him think this way. Perhaps he thought too highly of his position as a prophet to Israel and forgot God's desire to bless all nations—even Nineveh—through Israel. Or perhaps his personal prejudice against the people of Nineveh made him believe salvation was only for the Jews. Whatever the root, Jonah's heart isn't set on the things of God. The book of Jonah leaves us with Jonah sitting on that cliff above the city, feeling justified in his anger and unwilling to move, still hoping God might change His mind and smite the people of Nineveh.

Such a literary ending begs us to take a look at our own hearts. Are we being like Jonah? Are we waiting for something that isn't God's heart or His plan?

DAY 25: CHECK YOUR ATTITUDE

If we're going to wait well, we need to have an attitude check. Are there any areas in our lives where we're waiting for something that isn't in line with God's heart?

Let's not be like Jonah. Let's not let our bitterness, resentment, pride, or prejudice get in the way of God's blessing. I can't help but wonder how Jonah's story might have ended if instead of waiting for something that wasn't God's desire, Jonah rejoiced with the people who got to experience God's compassion and mercy.

In what ways have you seen God bless someone in your life with the thing you're waiting on? How did it make you feel to see them get that thing while you're still waiting?

Brainstorm some ways to celebrate with that person. How can you selflessly love on that person and celebrate God's blessing in their lives?

Take an attitude check. What thoughts are spinning around in your head about your waiting? What intentional choices or changes can you make today to change your attitude?

Day 26: Perfect Timing

Zechariah and Elizabeth

LUKE 1:5-25

It's fascinating to me how this thread of barrenness is woven throughout Scripture. From this vantage point—after studying the stories of Sarah, Rachel, and Hannah—I've come to view barrenness with expectation. Whenever Scripture draws attention to an emptiness—whether of a womb or something else—it takes me back to the beginning, to that point when nothing existed, but God's Spirit hovered and anticipation was high. Where there is emptiness, there is space for God to fill that barren place with something miraculous. This is the case with Elizabeth and Zechariah.

When we meet this couple in the first chapter of Luke, they are well along in years (Luke's words, not mine). The couple has likely seen much in life, having walked through several triumphs and joys together. Luke tells us that they are good people, "righteous in God's sight," (verse 6) and descendants of priestly families. They are the couple that did everything right, they followed the law, they were faithful, yet they were left wanting.

I don't know about you, but sometimes I think that God's willingness to deliver on a desire in my heart is dependent upon my behavior. If I do the right things and am obedient to Him, He'll come through.

In what ways in your waiting have you tried to use good behavior as a way to earn that thing you're waiting for?

I can't prove that this was something Elizabeth and Zechariah battled with, though it would definitely be a normal human response; but I do think it's fascinating that Luke is so detailed in outlining this couple's situation. It tells me that their childlessness isn't due to some fault of their own. Our author is setting us up to witness something miraculous.

As a member of the tribe of Levi, Zechariah is called upon to serve in the temple and burn incense before the Lord. This is a once in a lifetime opportunity, and some priests never get the chance. As he fulfills his duties, an angel shows up and delivers a message to Zechariah: "Do not be afraid, Zechariah, because your prayer has been heard. Your wife Elizabeth will bear you a son, and you will name him John" (verse 13).

I imagine that word from the Lord shook something inside Zechariah. He was well on in years and past the point of hoping for a child. Yet, here he stands with an angel telling him that the Lord is about to fulfill that desire. And not only that, but this promised child will be the forerunner to the Messiah. This little baby Elizabeth will give birth to will declare the coming of the Son of God and prepare the way for Jesus' ministry on earth.

DAY 26: PERFECT TIMING

Though Elizabeth and Zechariah may have given up on their desire for a child, God hadn't. The waiting was long and hard and there came a time when it felt like God's answer was "no," but that desire for a child was one God had planted in their hearts, and He fulfilled it at exactly the right time.

Sometimes God gives us a "no" answer for those things we're waiting for and when that happens we need to trust Him with that answer, believing that He has our best in mind. But sometimes what feels like a "no" because it hasn't happened yet is actually a future yes. It's an invitation to sit in the waiting a little longer and trust God's goodness. It's an invitation to remember that God sees the big picture and He knows the perfect timing. Sometimes God's perfect timing allows us to be part of something much bigger than we ever dreamed.

Have you reached the point of giving up on something you've waited for? What made you reach that point?

How do you feel about the idea that your wait may be tied in to something bigger God is doing?

What hope does Zechariah and Elizabeth's story provide in your season of waiting?

Day 27: Submitting to the Waiting

Mary

LUKE 1:26-38

IN THE WAITING

I've long admired Mary for her faith and her submission to God's will for her life. Mary's wait is an interesting one because her waiting wasn't something she asked for. Yesterday we looked at Zechariah and Elizabeth's wait for a child, and how God stepped in and finally declared the time was perfect to fulfill their long-held desire. When we meet Mary, however, she's a young Nazarene woman who is betrothed.

In the middle of her waiting for her betrothal period to end and her marriage to begin, the angel shows up and tells her that she will give birth to a little boy, the One who would be called the Son of the Most High. While the angel and his greeting startles her, she submits to the Lord's will and enters willingly into a season of unexpected waiting—waiting for a child she hasn't planned, but a child the whole nation of Israel has been waiting generations for.

Though she and Joseph aren't married in the sense that they live together and share a bed, a betrothal is a legally binding relationship. In Israel's culture, to be found pregnant outside of marriage was punishable by death. Mary knows the Law. She's aware of the consequences, but I believe she also has a solid love for God and belief in His goodness. If bearing a child is God's will, she is willing submit to it, but Mary risks a lot in her submission. She risks her marriage to Joseph, her acceptance in her community, and her very life.

I think that's why the angel greets her and calls her favored because God looks at her heart and sees a woman who will wait well for the promise He has given her. As an added bit of blessing and assurance, God passes on the news that Elizabeth, who had been barren, is pregnant too. When Mary travels to visit her cousin, her submission to God's will is rewarded with Elizabeth's words of blessing.

Read Luke 1:39-56. How does Elizabeth bless Mary?

The timing of all of this blows my mind because Elizabeth, who had waited so long for her heart's desire, gets to be an encouragement and a companion to Mary in her own waiting. It's a beautiful picture of community and mentoring that ushers Mary into a place of worship, as she praises God for all that He has done and will do.

Mary's was an unexpected wait, but when God spoke, she submitted. It hadn't been her plan to be the mother of the long-awaited Messiah, but by submitting and waiting for God's plans to come about, she was unexpectedly blessed. It was an opportunity to know God in new ways.

DAY 27: SUBMITTING TO THE WAITING

Whether the season of waiting you're in is for something you've planned for and wanted for a long time, or if it's a season you were thrown into because of something unexpected or maybe even painful, the best way to handle the waiting is to simply submit to it. Mary could have thrown out every reason possible as to why she couldn't be the woman for the job, but instead, she humbled herself and submitted to God's plans. In her submission, Mary experienced blessing. She experienced God in a new way and got to watch His promise of the Messiah be fulfilled right before her very eyes. She got to be part of that story.

Have you submitted to God in your season of waiting or are you fighting to get out of it?

Take a moment to humble yourself before the Lord and place the timeframe and the outcome of the waiting in God's hands. Write out Mary's words as your own prayer of submission.

Day 28: Reset Your Hope

Man at the Pool

JOHN 5:1-16

He'd already been there for a long time, this man by the pool. Over and over again the waters would stir and he would convince his body to move toward the pool, but inevitably someone else would get there first. Every. Single. Time.

Have you ever felt that way? That somehow your waiting is bound by time and you keep missing your window of opportunity?

I wonder how many years "a long time" is for this man. We're told that he's been disabled for thirty-eight years, but at what point did he start camping out by the pool, waiting for healing? How quickly into this new way of life did he stake his hope on this pool of water?

However long it's been, we can tell by the way he responds when Jesus shows up, that the man has just about run out of hope.

When Jesus notices the man and realizes his history—either because of His divine knowledge, or just the sure sign of the long years of waiting etched into the man's features—Jesus' question to the man is simple and straightforward: "Do you want to get well?" (verse 6).

As I read Scripture, especially stories of how Jesus interacts with people, the words come to life as pictures in my mind. I imagine the man hears Jesus' question and glances at Jesus for a moment before sighing and locking his eyes back on the pool he can never get to in time. His shoulders slump and his tone sounds resolved as the man replies, "Sir, I have no one to put me into the pool when the water is stirred up, but while I'm coming, someone goes down ahead of me" (verse 7).

Instead of responding to Jesus' question by saying that absolutely he wants to get well, the man lists all the obstacles in his way, all the ways he can't see that thing he's waited so long for actually becoming reality.

Not only is this man waiting for healing, but his response reveals a loneliness many of us experience in waiting seasons. We addressed this with Elijah's story a few days ago. This man is convinced he knows where his healing will come from, but he has no one to help him get there. It all just seems flat-out hopeless, but he stays because maybe, just maybe, one day it might not be so crowded and someone will notice him struggling and help him into the water.

DAY 28: RESET YOUR HOPE

Does hopeless feel like a word that describes your heart right now? How so?

I also can't help but wonder if the man's response is some kind of guarded request for Jesus to be the person to help him get to the pool. It's true that Jesus could have hung around until the waters stirred up then hustled the man to the water. But I think maybe Jesus' question was less about what the man wanted and more about getting a gauge on the man's heart. Jesus is an expert at reading between the lines of what a person says and what their soul actually needs. This man needs hope, but the hope he needs can't be found in a pool of water.

Rather than helping the man into the pool, Jesus does something greater. "Get up, pick up your mat and walk," Jesus says (verse 8).

With three brief commands, Jesus heals the man's body and restores his hope.

The pool of water was not his hope. Jesus was.

It's easy in seasons of waiting, especially when we've been waiting for a long time, like the man by the pool, to lose sight of the real source of our hope. Hope can easily get twisted to the point that we place all our hope on getting what we are waiting for, rather than on the One who can give us what we need. The man didn't need to get into the pool to be healed. All he needed was an encounter with Jesus.

We've talked a lot about what you're waiting for. You even wrote it all down on Day 1 before we dove into the study. But now I want to ask you a hard question: Why are you waiting for that thing? What do you think that thing will fix or give you if you were to get it?

Did that question raise your defenses a bit? That's okay. I'm not asking you this to make you feel bad or to condemn you for wanting. I'm not here to convince you to let go of that desire. Rather, I want to give you the opportunity to take a hard look at where you are placing your hope. If it's anywhere else besides Jesus, it's time to put your hope back in Him. Resetting your hope doesn't eliminate your desire. It simply means that whatever happens, your hope won't be shaken because it's not tied to what you're waiting for; it's tied to Jesus.

IN THE WAITING

Where are you placing your hope? Is it in the thing you are waiting for or is it in God?

What do you think this thing you want will fill or fix in your life if you get it?

How can you surrender that thing you are waiting on to God today and let Him be your hope?

Day 29: Want the Right Thing

The 5,000
JOHN 6:1-40

IN THE WAITING

Everyone likes a good miracle. We like it when God shows up and shows off, and we especially like when He answers our prayers just the way we want. When we get that thing we've been waiting on, we celebrate, and when we don't get it, we keep trudging through the season of waiting, eyes locked on that thing we don't yet have.

The problem many of us face in seasons of waiting is that we can get so caught up in wanting that we lose sight of God. Remember, we want to draw near to God in the waiting, not drift away from Him. But if we're honest, sometimes we want "it" more than we want Him.

That's what happened with the 5,000 people Jesus fed. He had compassion on them and provided for their needs, but when the people walked away with full bellies, they decided to follow Him the next day and see what else this Jesus guy could do. They became addicted to the miracles and wanted to see another one. Not to mention, Jesus could make some pretty tasty bread.

Of course, Jesus saw right through that and called the people out on their true motives. He knew they hadn't come for Him, but for what He could do for them. The people weren't really hearing Him, though. Instead, they tried to manipulate the conversation to get what they wanted from Jesus.

Look again at verses 26-35. In your own words, summarize this conversation. What is Jesus trying to communicate?

That thing you're waiting for, it's not eternal. We've touched on this in a previous day, but in my own waiting, I've learned that when my emotions and desires are tied up tightly into a thing I want God to do for me, sometimes I need to hear something multiple times before I begin to understand. This isn't to discourage you, but I hope it makes you stop and assess how you're wanting is affecting your relationship with Jesus. We have to be careful not to place the object of our want as a higher priority than knowing God in the waiting. Wanting is fine. We're allowed to want; but as soon as we want something more than we want God, that's an idol, and like the crowd of 5,000, we miss the point.

Don't limit your interactions with the Lord to that thing you want. Ask Him for it, that's fine. In fact, He invites us to ask. And when you ask, sit back and watch for Him to answer, but don't neglect to seek the Lord for the simple pleasure of knowing Him better. Seek God for God rather than for what you can get from Him. Remember, faith is about relationship.

DAY 29: WANT THE RIGHT THING

Get to know the Lord and allow Him to reveal Himself to you as the One who is more than just a miracle performer. He is God and He desires relationship.

Take a heart check. Are you really seeking to know God better, or do you just want Him to do things for you? Confess and ask God to set your heart right.

What is one simple thing you can do to spend time with God today?

Day 30: Dealing with Distraction

Peter

MATTHEW 14:22-23

IN THE WAITING

I've often wondered why Jesus sends the disciples on ahead in the boat after feeding the 5,000. We know that He went off on His own for a while and He planned on catching up with the others later, but I have to wonder how much the Holy Spirit revealed to Jesus about the next few hours. Was this a planned thing to increase their faith? I also can't help but wonder what the disciples thought about the whole ordeal, being caught in the storm after seeing a miracle just a few hours before.

From an outsider's perspective, looking in on this story, I want to blame Jesus for the struggle the disciples endured. They were following His instructions when He sent them on ahead. Because of Him, whether He knew about the storm or not, they were beaten by the waves and fought against the winds.

If I'm honest, sometimes I blame the Lord for the storms I face in the waiting too. Didn't He know this would be hard and painful? Didn't He know I would feel beaten down by the struggles and fight against the winds of doubt and uncertainty?

Do you relate to this in any way?

After a long day of ministry, now the disciples must battle against the elements. Yet it's in the middle of the storm that Jesus shows up, walking on top of the churning waves. The hard winds have no effect on Him. His steps are steady, His way smooth, even though every element around Him is far from calm. It's in this storm that Peter sees Jesus and asks to be called out onto the waves with Him, and Jesus invites Peter out.

We give Peter so much grief for doubting, for taking his eyes off Jesus and panicking when he begins to sink, but we forget to celebrate his faith. Before the wind and waves got the better of him, Peter, for a brief moment, was not tossed by the storm. He walked on water. He had his eyes fixed on Jesus and was walking with Him on top of the waves, unaffected by the wind. Peter only begins to sink when he gets distracted by all the chaos around him.

While waiting seasons are often compared to desert wastelands, these seasons are also prime conditions for storms and struggles. These are the seasons where, despite those areas where we believe we are following God's leading and direction, chaos happens, things fall apart, and we get slammed. It might be tempting in those times to abandon ship or allow our hearts to become bitter and blame God for the hardships we face. But in those times, we need to remember that He has not abandoned us or sent us off on our own. He is walking among the waves and invites us out onto the water with Him.

DAY 30: DON'T GET DISTRACTED

Don't let life's storms distract you in the waiting. Instead, trust the One who walks with you in the storm. Keep your eyes locked on Him and trust Him to deliver you to the other side.

In what ways does life feel stormy or chaotic right now?

What would it take for you to lift your eyes from all of the distractions and fix your eyes on the Lord?

Day 31: Sit With Jesus

Martha and Mary

LUKE 10:38-42

I've read and heard a lot of teaching on this passage of Scripture. Whenever a pastor or teacher lists this reference and tells us we're going to be digging into the story of Mary and Martha, I roll my eyes a little. The eye-rolling is in part because this story is so familiar, but also because most of the time when it's taught, Martha is painted in a bad light. It's usually all very black and white: Be a Mary, not a Martha. Stop doing so much. Don't make serving your aim. Instead, sit at Jesus' feet. And that message is in there, but it's not the only lesson we can glean from this story. In fact, I think there is something Martha can teach us about how to draw near to God in seasons of wanting.

There is a lot going on the day Jesus shows up at Martha's house. She welcomes Him and His followers in and then sets about making sure they are comfortable, fed, and provided for. She is doing what any good hostess would do. But under the surface of her hospitality, she is also a little bitter because she is doing all of the work alone. Mary should be helping, but where is she? Not in the kitchen, but sitting at Jesus' feet listening, learning, spending time with Him.

I don't know that it would be too much of a stretch to say that perhaps Martha's so irked at her sister's absence from the kitchen because Martha wants to be at Jesus' feet too. Perhaps she thinks that if Mary were helping, they could get the work done and Martha could rest and listen to Jesus.

In seasons of waiting, I think that is often the goal isn't it? We just want to get through it and get it done and over with. There are waiting seasons where we're called to rest and not act, but many of our waiting seasons require action and work, preparation and learning, and living faithfully right where we are. It's hard to shake the idea that once we get through this thing, once we reach our goal, once God answers, we can finally rest at Jesus' feet. We can finally take a breather and put our feet up and rest for a moment from all the work.

But the key to waiting well and drawing near to God in those seasons is learning how to sit at Jesus' feet while you're still waiting. Martha wanted Mary's help, but Mary knew something her sister hadn't quite caught on to—something I still have trouble pressing into—that the work will still be there. What we actually need isn't to push through, but to stop and sit with Jesus for a while.

Notice how Jesus responds to Martha when she asks Him to tell Mary to help her: "Martha, Martha, you are worried and upset about many things, but one thing is necessary. Mary has made the right choice, and it will not be taken away from her" (verses 41-42).

What is Jesus calling Martha out on? What is His concern here?

DAY 31: SIT WITH JESUS

Most teachings will call attention to the fact that Martha was too focused on her work, but Jesus doesn't address Martha's work. He calls her out on her worries.

There is a lot to worry about when you're waiting. Will the waiting ever end? Does God even care about my desires? Am I waiting well or do I need to do something different? Should I try harder or should I stop waiting all together? Is God actually going to come through?

We also know that waiting can sometimes mean working. Remember Noah? But there are times when waiting means putting the work and the worries aside so that we can press deeper into relationship with Jesus. And that relationship is not built on striving, but resting and trusting the One who waits with us.

One of the simplest things we can do to draw near to God in seasons of wanting is to just sit with Him. Plop down at His feet and listen. Let go of the to-do list. Let go of the worries. Let go of your need to remind Him that you're still waiting on that one thing. Just sit. Sit and listen. Be in His presence.

What worries are you carrying right now in the waiting?

How can you choose the right thing and sit at Jesus' feet today?

Day 32: Seek Him Out

Zacchaeus

LUKE 19:1-10

IN THE WAITING

Most likely, if you're familiar with Zacchaeus, it's because you heard about him in Sunday School. Maybe the song is playing in your head now: *Zacchaeus was a wee little man and a wee little man was he...*

When you think about stories of those who waited, it's likely that Zacchaeus isn't the first person to come to your mind—or even the fifteenth. Waiting feels like a long, drawn out process that can be mildly traumatic, and we've seen that with many of the people we've studied. They waited years, decades, or even generations. They dealt with doubt, disappointment, and dead desires. Zacchaeus's story doesn't involve any of that.

So why is his story part of this study? Because I think Zacchaeus is an excellent example of someone who exemplifies waiting in expectation.

Remember our lesson from the beginning—the literal beginning of life in Genesis 1:1 that we looked at on Day 2? What was the message about waiting?

Waiting doesn't always have to be traumatic. In fact, the origin of waiting is based in anticipation and expectancy—two things Zacchaeus can teach us about.

When Luke introduces Zacchaeus to us, we learn a few things about him.

Glance back at today's passage. What do you learn about Zacchaeus from Luke's introduction of him?

As a result of his occupation as a tax collector, Zacchaeus is a man with wealth and position. Tax collectors at that time worked for Rome, and the Jews who served in that line of work weren't highly thought of. Rome already left a bitter taste in the mouths of the Jews, but many tax collectors used their position to charge their community members more than was required and pocket the extra. Their extortion only added to the people's dislike of them.

DAY 32: SEEK HIM OUT

This is the kind of man Luke introduces us to. Zacchaeus is a cheat, a liar, and a traitor in the eyes of his community.

But we also learn two other important things about this man—that he is short and that he's trying to see Jesus.

Like so many other people by this point in Jesus' ministry, Zacchaeus has heard about Jesus. So when Zacchaeus learns that Jesus is passing through Jericho, he makes sure to catch a glimpse. In fact, if we zoom out from our passage and look at the larger context, it's likely that Zacchaeus has caught word of a miracle that happened just outside the city.

Read Luke 18:35-43. What happened outside of Jericho?

Such a miracle, in addition to whatever else Zacchaeus has heard about Jesus, makes the short tax collector eager to see this man of miracles. Though the crowd hinders Zacchaeus's view of Jesus, he's determined enough to throw aside his pride for a moment to run ahead of the group, climb a tree, and wait for Jesus to pass by.

If this story had played out differently, if Zacchaeus hadn't put forth that extra effort and climbed the tree to see Jesus, we wouldn't know who he is. It makes me wonder if Jesus would have spotted Zacchaeus peeking over shoulders. Would Jesus have called him out of the crowd? Would He still have invited Himself over to Zacchaeus' house for dinner?

Truthfully, I don't know what would have been. What I do know is that Zacchaeus' effort and his determination to see Jesus was rewarded. Not only was he able to see Jesus from his perch in that tree, but his efforts to see Jesus led to a more intimate encounter with Jesus over a meal, and it changed Zacchaeus's life. Zacchaeus could have just as easily kept his head down and focused on his work, focused on getting what he wanted out of the people, but he didn't. He left his table and went looking for Jesus.

This short and slightly humorous story makes me wonder what might happen if we put a little more effort into trying to see Jesus. I wonder how the waiting seasons would look if we did what Zacchaeus did and set ourselves up to watch for Jesus. I'm not talking about watching for Him to do what we're waiting for Him to do. Watch for that, yes, but don't let your desire for what He will do distract from what He is already doing.

It's easy in our waiting to keep our heads down, focus on the task at hand, focus on getting what we want from God. When that happens, we need to pull a Zacchaeus and get a better vantage point. We need to put forth some effort and seek Jesus out. Now, let me be clear here that this doesn't mean we try harder or do more. It simply means that we have to adjust our priorities. We have to put ourselves in a position to see Him at work.

Zacchaeus was expectant. He wanted something—to see Jesus—and he took steps to make that happen. He didn't sit at his table and wait for Jesus to come to him. He sought out Jesus. If we're going to draw near to the Lord in seasons of waiting, sometimes we have to be the ones to pursue Him and seek Him out. God is always pursuing us, but He will never force relationship on us. He gives us the dignity and freedom to choose to pursue Him. Sometimes we have to go the extra mile—or climb the proverbial tree—to get a good view of Him, to see above the distractions that even our own waiting can cause.

What lengths are you going to so that you can see and be with Jesus in your waiting?

How does Zacchaeus's story encourage you in your waiting?

Day 33: Coming to the End of Yourself

The Bleeding Woman

LUKE 8:40-56

IN THE WAITING

While the bleeding woman is our focus today, at first glance, this passage doesn't seem to be about her at all. It begins with a father named Jairus, who seeks out Jesus to ask Him to come heal his dying daughter. As Jesus is traveling to Jairus' house, the bleeding woman interrupts their journey and reaches for the edge of Jesus' robe, confident that if she can just touch Jesus, she will get the one thing every other doctor had failed to give her—healing.

Her condition has plagued her body for twelve years. Having a chronic illness is hard for anyone, but her particular condition comes with extra complications.

Jewish law states that a woman with a bleeding disorder is to be separated from the community (Leviticus 15:25). Because of this law, the bleeding woman is considered unclean and anything or anyone who comes in contact with her also becomes unclean and unable to worship at the temple. Every bit of money this woman has been able to scrape together has gone toward any kind of solution she could find, but everything she's tried yielded no results (Mark 5:26).

This woman is isolated, desperate, and out of options. If doctors can't fix her, she is destined to live out the rest of her life alone and unclean.

Then one day Jesus passes by on the street and she sees an opportunity. She's heard the stories about this man, even as she's kept her distance from people. She knows what He is capable of, and she truly has nothing to lose. She won't ask Him for anything. She won't make Him stop or cause a scene. Her plan is just to slip through the crowd quietly, touch His robe, and be on her way. Jesus will never notice her in such a crowd.

Or so she thinks.

What is Jesus' response to being touched?

After the woman's brief point of contact with Jesus' robe, Jesus stops and asks the crowd who touched Him. It's a silly question, as the disciples point out, since they're caught in a crowd and everyone is touching. Jesus, however, is clear that His inquiry isn't about finding a person who had jostled or bumped Him. The touch, He explains to His perplexed disciples, had been an intentional one, and He felt the power go out of Him.

The woman felt it too. As soon as she touched Him, her bleeding stopped. She was healed! And petrified. Because now Jesus is calling her out. Trembling, she falls on her knees before Jesus and tells Him her story about her years of waiting, all the ways she has tried to find

DAY 33: THE END OF YOURSELF

a cure for her illness, her belief that just a touch of the hem of Jesus' tunic would heal her, and that it had. Perhaps her trembling is caused by her fear of being reprimanded. Truly, she shouldn't even be among these people, and she definitely shouldn't have touched any of them. But instead of condemning her, Jesus reaches out a kind hand, helps the woman back to her feet and speaks words that are balm for her soul: "Daughter, your faith has healed you. Go in peace" (verse 48).

Healing. Peace. Two words this woman has waited over a decade for, and now they are finally available to her. She'd come to the end of herself. She had reached out in hope and expectation, and that hope was rewarded.

There comes a point in the waiting where you have spent everything you've got. Financially. Emotionally. Your time. Your hope. Your options. Your opportunities. Everything has dried up and you've got nothing, absolutely nothing left. As hard as it is, I think sometimes maybe that is the point of the waiting. We have to get to get to the end of ourselves. We have to get to the end of all of our trying to make it happen on our own. We have to get to the end of our own solutions and schemes. Heck, I think we even need to get to the end of our belief that the object of our wait will fix things. We need to get to the point where we realize all of that other stuff we've been trying in order to end our wait doesn't work and we're left with just Jesus. Maybe Jesus feels like our last hope, but really, He's our only hope.

In what ways do you feel at the end of your rope in the waiting? What have you tried to do to end your waiting and how did that turn out?

What do you think the difference would be in changing our mindset from seeing Jesus as our last hope to our only hope?

IN THE WAITING

How is the Lord challenging you from today's study?

Day 34: Waiting and Grieving

Mary of Bethany

JOHN 11:1-44

I can relate to Mary's grief and brokenness. She did what she knew to do—she sent a message to Jesus, letting Him know that her brother was dying. She put her faith in Him, and He didn't show.

Not until it was too late.

Not until her brother was four-days-dead and lying in a tomb.

On this side of Mary's story, we know those four days Lazarus lay in the tomb served a purpose. We know that those four days made way for Jesus' greatest miracle yet and foreshadowed what would happen to Jesus. Those four days symbolize how we are dead in our sins until Jesus raises us to new life in Him (Ephesians 2:1-10). Those ideas are aspects and stories of our faith that we celebrate. But Mary was caught in the middle of what felt like the end. She had no way of knowing what kind of miracle lay ahead. Her hope was buried with her brother in the grave, and all she held was a handful of broken faith.

Mary had put her hope in Jesus. She'd tended to her brother in his illness and sent a message to their friend Jesus when Lazarus took a turn for the worst. Mary fully believed Lazarus would live if she could just get him to Jesus. She knew what Jesus was capable of, and when He showed up too late, it broke her heart.

She is so grieved by the whole ordeal, this woman who is praised for sitting at Jesus' feet, that she doesn't go out to greet Him. When her sister Martha rushes to meet Jesus on the road, Mary stays in the dimly lit home with the other mourners. It's not until Martha returns with news that Jesus is asking for her, that Mary goes and falls at His feet and weeps, her grief pouring out onto the dusty ground.

"Lord, if you had been here, my brother wouldn't have died!" (verse 32).

It always amazes me how Jesus meets each person according to their need. Unlike how He met Martha, Jesus doesn't give an explanation or enter into a theological discussion. He doesn't use logic or the language of resurrection. Instead, He meets Mary in her sorrow and weeps with her.

The reality is, not everything we're waiting on is going to turn out like we hope. I know I've said this a lot already, but I want to be clear because it would be easy for me to mislead you. I don't want to give you a false hope that God is definitely going to come through on that thing you're waiting for. If He's promised, you can trust Him to be faithful. But that thing you're waiting on is just a hope or a desire you're holding on to, He may do it or He may not. We don't know how things will turn out, so we keep hoping, but we do so with open hands, ready to receive whatever God's answer is, whenever He gives it, and while we wait, we draw near to Him.

Mary's story does have a happy and miraculous ending. While she waited for her brother to be healed and didn't get what she wanted, she did get to see her four-days-dead brother

DAY 34: WAITING AND GRIEVING

raised back to life. It wasn't too late after all. Jesus did come through. It just wasn't like she had hoped, and it was certainly not in the timing she had intended.

Too often we skip over the heaviness of the disappointment and grief to get to the miracle, but I think sitting in this part of Mary's story—before the miracle, when she thought it was over—is important too because the reality is that sometimes that thing we're waiting on dies. We may not experience a physical death, like what Mary experienced with her brother. It could be a death of a dream, a job, a relationship, or our plans. When that happens, we may wonder where God is, why He doesn't show up and move. We may wonder why He doesn't give us a miracle. We may rail at the heavens, begging God to speak. But one thing I learn about the Lord from Mary's story is that those deaths and tragedies break His heart too. While He may seem silent and distant, He's never left us. He doesn't let us grieve alone; He even grieves with us.

Jesus wept with Mary and He weeps with us too.

Sometimes the deaths we experience are actual ends and He walks with us through that. Other times, those deaths are opportunities for Him to raise up something new out of the ashes. Sometimes those things we thought were dead gain new life.

If you're in the hard part of the waiting, the part where you've called on God and it looks like He just isn't going to show up—if it feels like it's too late—keep waiting. Be honest with God about what you're feeling. Share your grief, your anger, your frustration and disappointment with Him. The Lord isn't finished yet. Even if this particular thing has died, something new can spring to life from it.

How do you find yourself relating to Mary's waiting?

What does it mean to you to know that God is grieves with you when things you've been waiting for die?

IN THE WAITING

What might it look like for you to grieve with the Lord about your waiting?

Day 35: Worth It

Jesus

LUKE 22:39-53

IN THE WAITING

Jesus waited.

Part of me is surprised by that statement. It's a true one, but I think sometimes I lean more heavily on Jesus' divinity and forget about His humanity. He was both God and man, and while He was able to multiply bread and fish, calm storms, and heal people, Jesus also experienced human stuff, like waiting.

It's weird, at least for me, to wrap my mind around, but it also brings me a little bit of peace. Sometimes waiting can feel more like God is somehow outside of our waiting rather than in it with us. The truth is that He knows all about waiting, and as we head toward the final days of this study, I hope that today's lesson gives you peace and convinces you just how close the Lord is and how well acquainted He is with the weight of waiting.

Long before His prayer in Gethsemane, Jesus was waiting. His waiting began the day humanity was exiled from Eden.

Read Genesis 3:22-24. How did the Lord's waiting begin?

On the first read of this Genesis passage it sounds like God doesn't want humanity to live forever, but go back and read it again in light of Creation and the original intent for humanity and you'll find that this isn't about keeping man from living forever, but keeping man from living forever *in a fallen state*. If humanity would experience eternity, God wanted us to do so as wholly restored beings, not broken and sinful ones. The day Adam and Eve are sent out of the Garden, the Lord sets a plan in motion. He calls Abraham and makes a promise.

We spent some time looking at this thread of covenant when we studied David and how so many of the waiting stories we find in Scripture are connected to Abraham's wait. We see that from a human perspective. But what happens if we change the point of view and look at it from God's perspective?

Do you remember what the promise was God made to Abraham? Look back at Genesis 12:1-3 if you need a refresher. How might seeing this covenant from God's perspective change how you understand it?

DAY 35: WORTH IT

Through Abraham a nation is birthed. As the generations continue, God leads His people out of slavery and into a new way of living. When they rebel against having God as their king and demand they have a king like all the other nations, God raises up a dynasty through whom He promises ultimate redemption will come.

That is where God's covenant with David comes in. Do you remember the promise God made to David? (Look back at 2 Samuel 7:12-16 if you need a refresher.)

After David, generations passed and a special baby boy, promised to a young virgin, is born in a stable in Bethlehem. That baby grows into a perfect man who is also the Son of God, and after three years of teaching, healing, and performing miracles, He ends up here in a Garden late at night, waiting.

Waiting for His betrayal.

Waiting for one man who is both a friend and disciple to kiss his check and sentence Him to death.

Waiting for this long story of covenant and restored relationship with humanity to reach its climax.

Over the next few hours, Jesus would be arrested, beaten, mocked, hung on a cross, and buried in a tomb.

If we settle into this story right here where He knows He is headed to death, it begs the question, was all of His waiting worth it? Was it worth generations of waiting and building up the nation of Israel? Was it worth all the times the people turned against Him? Was it worth the pain and agony and rejection He faced while on earth?

The cross wants to convince me it was all a waste of time, but the empty tomb tells me otherwise.

Yes, Jesus is fully God, but He is also fully man. He felt the weight of waiting. He felt the weight, not only of His earthly waiting, but He also felt the weight of every generation since Eden. No one knows about waiting better than the One who gave His own life to win us back.

IN THE WAITING

I don't have to guess about what Jesus' answer would be if we asked Him if He thought all that waiting was worth it. I know what He would say: Of course it was worth it. It was worth all of the time, agony, pain, suffering, and rejection because in all of that painful waiting Jesus accomplished something so mind-blowingly amazing.

Read Romans 5:6-8. What does this passage reveal about Jesus' wait?

At the right time, the perfect time, the time He had planned, Jesus came and gave His life so that we could live forever in relationship with Him. Whole. Healed. Wholly His.

Jesus knows about waiting. It may be tempting to distance yourself from Him or see Him as the cause of your waiting, but Jesus is the best partner to have in seasons of waiting. He is well acquainted with not yet having what you want and taking steps to get it. He's well aware of how other people's choices affect us in the waiting. He is also a great comfort and encourager to remind us that no matter how hard or painful or long the waiting is, it's always worth it. Like a mother holding her newborn baby, I want to get to the end of the wait, whether I have what I want or not, and I want to say that it was worth it. I see that in Jesus' story. I want to see it in my own too.

How does knowing that Jesus waited encourage you in your own weight?

What have your opinions been about Him in regards to waiting? Have you blamed Him for it or have you used it as a way to connect with Him at a deeper level?

DAY 35: WORTH IT

What would make all of this waiting worth it for you?

Day 36: Room for Doubt

Thomas

JOHN 20:19-29

Thomas might be my favorite disciple. Peter gets a lot of air time because of his boldness, John is often a quiet favorite, but Thomas is generally only remembered for his doubt. "Doubting Thomas" is what they call him. How would you like to have a reputation like that? When his story is taught, it's often with the lesson that we're not supposed to be like Thomas, but I think we're doing Thomas a disservice by only looking at his story as a model of what not to do. There is actually quite a bit he could teach us about faith when we're in a season of waiting.

Doubt feels like a taboo word. We're taught to have faith and that there is not room for doubt in faith. I think that's a misconception. I believe doubt can become fertile ground from which our faith can grow.

Doubt by definition is a feeling of uncertainty. Uncertainty can lead us in one of two directions. It can either spur us forward to find answers, or it can be the place where we turn around in unbelief. Doubt is a middle place, a fork in the road. It is the place we sit in to decide where we go from here. Doubt itself isn't bad. It's an opportunity.

I think God has a soft spot for doubters. The reason I believe this is because, rather than condemning Thomas for his doubt, Jesus shows up in the middle of it.

Thomas missed out on Jesus' first appearance to the disciples. Wherever he was, when he returned to that upper room, he did not believe what the disciples were telling him. They had seen Jesus. He was alive! But Thomas wasn't a guy who simply believed everything he heard, especially not something like this. Grief had made his friends hopeful and perhaps a little delusional. People didn't rise from the dead. Sure, Jesus had raised Lazarus and the son of a widow (Luke 7:11-17), but raising oneself from death was completely idiotic. No, Thomas would not base his faith just on words, even though those words came from the men and women he had spent the last few years traveling with. He had seen Jesus arrested. Word spread quickly about His death. If Jesus was really alive, Thomas would have to see Him with his own eyes. He would have to touch Jesus' wounds.

For Thomas, seeing and touching was linked with belief. His doubt didn't stem from unbelief. Maybe it's a stretch, but I think he wanted to believe. Like the other disciples, Thomas had seen Jesus do amazing things. He'd spent time learning at Jesus' feet and believed there was something divine about Him. But in his grief, Thomas had doubts. He wanted proof. Why else would he make the statement about putting his fingers in Jesus' wounds?

Instead of reprimanding Thomas for doubting, Jesus shows up and offers His hands with their nail-pierced wounds for Thomas to touch. He shows Thomas His side and invites him to touch the wound left by the spear. Jesus shows up again for the sake of Thomas, to reconcile his doubt and help him to believe. Without even making a move, the disciple falls on his knees and declares his faith: "My Lord and my God!" (verse 28).

In the waiting, if you haven't encountered it already, it's likely that you will face a season of doubt. You will wonder if God will come through, if He'll do what He said, if you'll see what He has promised. You will doubt, and that's okay. It doesn't disqualify your faith. Doubting simply gives us another opportunity to get honest with God and ask Him to prove Himself again—to remind us of His faithfulness, His presence, and His goodness.

It's okay to doubt and it's okay to ask for proof. Yes, believing when you don't see is amazing and definitely a huge part of faith. Hebrews 11:1 tells us that. But I think sometimes people use that verse to chase away the doubt. As soon as we feel even an inkling of doubt rising up in us, because we've been taught doubt is wrong, we push it away and try to muster up more faith. Thomas's story gives us permission to embrace the doubt. Instead running from it, we're invited to enter into our doubt and meet God in the middle of it.

Don't run away from your doubt. Don't try to muster up enough faith to believe God. He knows your heart. Your doubt does not scare Him. It might be tempting in the doubt to distance yourself, to think it's not acceptable in a life of faith, but don't. Instead, ask Him to show Himself to you. Ask Him to come through. Allow your doubt to feed your faith. We're human and sometimes we just need some proof. God knows that sometimes we need something tangible and visible, something to hold onto in this time of wanting. He showed up for Thomas. He'll show up for you too.

What doubts are you carrying right now?

How could you use your doubt as a way to draw near to God?

Day 37: Praying While You Wait

The Disciples
ACTS 1:1-2:4

IN THE WAITING

Before Jesus ascended into heaven, He gave His disciples one last command. They were instructed not to leave Jerusalem. He told them stay put, to "wait for the Father's promise" (Acts 1:4). That promise was the coming of the Holy Spirit.

Before the crucifixion Jesus had taught His disciples about the Holy Spirit.

Read John 14:15-26. What does Jesus teach His disciples about the Holy Spirit and what His role will be in the lives of those who follow Him?

Throughout Scripture there is a thread you can follow from beginning to end that shows God continuing to draw near to His people. He did that in the Garden. Before everything fell apart, God would walk with Adam and Eve in the cool of the evening. He drew near when He called Abraham and singled out his family as the ones through whom blessing would come to everyone. God revealed His presence at Mount Sinai and allowed His presence to dwell in the Tabernacle at the center of Israel's camp, during their wandering years. God came even closer when He took on flesh and came to earth as a baby and spent some time walking around in the world He'd created.

Now, with the promise of the Holy Spirit, God is getting ready to take another step closer. In order to receive that promise, though, and to experience God in this new, more intimate way, the disciples had to stop staring up at the sky, return to the city, and wait.

We've focused a lot of our attention throughout this study on stories that have involved active waiting. Noah built an ark. Gideon laid out a fleece. Esther gathered her community. The bleeding woman reached out her hand. Zacchaeus climbed a tree. That's not really the case here. The disciples were told to stay where they were. That was the only action they were given.

Waiting seasons aren't as difficult to manage when we're able to be active in some way. It's the sitting-still-and-staying-put kind of waiting that gets challenging. Being still and staying put can feel excruciatingly hard. We want to do something, make progress, make it happen. But sometimes there is nothing we can do but wait.

When it came to understanding how and when their waiting would end, the disciples knew very little. They didn't know how long they were to stay in the city and wait. They didn't know exactly what day Holy Spirit would show up or how they would know when the Holy Spirit arrived and their waiting was complete. They faced so many unknowns. But

DAY 37: PRAYING WHILE YOU WAIT

you know what they did during this time when they were instructed to stay put? They prayed together. They stayed in communication with God. They asked God to do what Jesus had promised. They worshiped, listened, and sat silently together. They devoted themselves to prayer.

It may not seem like much, and perhaps praying for any length of time feels just as bad as sitting still and doing nothing, but here's something I am fully convinced of: that time of prayer prepared the disciples to receive the Holy Spirit and notice when He showed up.

The disciples made use of that time gathered together in that space to establish some structure in their community. Judas Iscariot was gone from their group and they had a spot to fill, so they prayed and asked God to show them who should fill the twelfth spot and Matthias was chosen.

The disciples weren't given any tasks to complete while they waited. They could have chosen any number of ways to fill their time while they stayed in Jerusalem, but they chose to spend it in prayer and communal waiting. They chose to follow the example Jesus had given them while He was on earth and spent time communing with the Father.

Waiting wasn't just an empty space for the disciples. They used that time well. They prayed and the set up a new structure so that when Jesus' words were fulfilled, they were ready to move.

Waiting can feel like a tedious burden, but if we allow it, it can be a rich time, especially when we bathe that waiting space in prayer.

What kind of waiting are you in the midst of? Is it the kind that requires action and work, or the kind where God has asked you to stay put?

How can you invest yourself in prayer in this season? What is God inviting you to pray about?

IN THE WAITING

Are there any routines, habits, or structures in your life that you can work on developing so that you are ready to move when the waiting is done?

Day 38: Sufficient Grace

Paul

2 CORINTHIANS 12:1-10

IN THE WAITING

One of the hardest things about waiting is when God finally answers and His answer is no. We've seen a lot of "yes" answers over the last several weeks. Some of those yeses were quick, others came after years of painful longing, but we haven't seen very many nos. Jonah got a hard no when God dished out mercy instead of condemnation on the people of Nineveh, but that "no" feels a little easier to accept. After all, Jonah's attitude was off. He was well aware of God's mercy and didn't want Nineveh to receive it. In that situation, I can support God's answer.

God's answer to Paul, however, is a little harder to deal with.

Paul has one of the most dramatic conversation stories recorded in Scripture. Trained as a Pharisee, he used his influence and education to arrest and kill followers of Jesus. He was on his way to purge another town of Christians when Jesus encountered Paul on the road. Paul was never the same after that experience. From that point on he became an apostle of Jesus, sharing the Gospel, and bringing the Good News to those outside of the Jewish community. He faced a lot of persecution and his life was often in danger. Then, somewhere along the way, he picked up a thorn. We don't know what exactly that thorn was. It wasn't a literal thorn, but it was something that bugged him, something that irritated him or caused him enough pain that he asked God three times to take it away from him.

God told Paul, "No."

The fascinating thing about God's response to Paul's request, though, is that God does provide a solution, it just wasn't the one Paul had asked for.

What solution does God give Paul in verse 9?

Instead of relief, God gave Paul endurance. Instead of strengthening Paul, God gave him the opportunity to lean into His power. God knew what Paul didn't yet know when he asked God to remove the thorn—that it was actually Paul's weakness that would draw him closer to God and make him more effective in ministry. Whatever ailed Paul, its presence required him to lean heavily on God, to rely on His power and strength to make up for Paul's weaknesses. But it was in those weaknesses that Paul found true strength.

Seeing Paul's response to how his waiting ended, I have to wonder how willing we are to receive a no answer from God. We've been digging into Scripture and taking steps to draw near to God in our wanting. We've moved through with hope that God would come

DAY 38: SUFFICIENT GRACE

through and answer, but what if His answer is no? What if He decides to move differently than the way we want Him to? How do we respond then?

First, I think we need to grieve. While Scripture doesn't say it, I'm almost certain Paul had to deal with some level of grief over God's answer. By the time Paul writes this letter to the church at Corinth, he's accepted God's answer, but it's likely it took him some time to get to this point. He is human, after all, and a no answer, even when we accept it as God's best and as grace, still requires time to process the disappointment and even the grief, and that's okay.

When we're waiting and hoping for God to do something specific, we invest a lot of ourselves and our emotions in that waiting, so we're going to have to give ourselves space and time to grieve when things don't turn out like we hoped. When that happens, we have a God who will grieve with us. Allow God into the grief. Tell Him about your disappointment and anger and all the other raw emotions you have. Allow the hard no to draw you closer to Him.

We need to recognize that God is very intentional in His no answers. No might feel like a cruel answer, like He's holding out on us or denying us something. It may feel like He doesn't love us, but that is far from true. God is our Father and He always does what is best, even if His idea of best is different from ours. It is okay to open up conversation with Him, to ask Him how no is the best thing. Simply asking *Why is this best, Lord? How does this no help further your kingdom?* can go a long way in helping us draw near to Him even when the answer isn't what we wanted.

The lesson we learn from Paul's story is that no matter the outcome of our waiting season, God's grace is always sufficient. In unanswered prayers, when the answer is no, or when we're still having to deal with the thing we hoped God would take away, His grace is sufficient. His undeserved favor is still upon us. His blessing still comes, even if it comes in unexpected ways.

When God gives us a no, it doesn't mean He loves us any less. In fact, it means quite the opposite. It means He loves us enough to tell us no, and perhaps that is the kindest avenue of grace.

Has God's answer to your current waiting or a past season of waiting been no? How did you respond to that?

IN THE WAITING

What do you fear most if God's answer to your waiting is no?

How do you see God's grace as sufficient in your life right now?

Day 39: The End of Waiting

New Creation
REVELATION 21-22

It seems only fitting that the way we began this study is the way we end it—with Creation. In the beginning, God's Spirit hovered over the face of the deep. Where there was nothing there was anticipation for what God was about to do. Waiting got twisted, though, when sin entered the world. Ever since then, all of Creation has been longing for the fulfillment of God's great rescue plan, when the earth, humanity, and our relationship with God would be set completely right again (Romans 8:18-25).

It doesn't matter what we're waiting for, all of us, across all generations, are ultimately waiting for God's kingdom. We're waiting for complete restoration and redemption so that sin no longer hinders, death no longer claims those we love, and pain is no longer part of life.

We're waiting for New Creation, and in Revelation we see the promise of the fulfillment of that longing.

Take some time to reflect on today's Scripture reading. What verses stuck out to you? What emotions or longings does this passage raise for you? What hope does it encourage?

Revelation has a lot of weird stuff in it that is often hard to understand, but these final two chapters awaken a deep hope in the human heart and remind us that ultimately, all of our waiting will be worth it.

In this life we'll go through seasons of waiting and wanting. We'll see God answer. We will celebrate and grieve and move forward into yet another waiting season. In between all of our waiting for things to change, for healing to happen, and dreams to become reality, there is this continuing thread of waiting that knits us all together with everyone who has ever lived and will ever live. We are waiting for what we know in our souls to be true—that this world isn't right, but it can and will be. One day. This soul-desire for the world to be set right again will be answered when Jesus returns to establish the new heaven and new earth.

New Creation is coming. These two chapters at the very end of the Bible assure us of that. They promise fulfillment. They promise that God will give a resounding yes to the ache inside all of us. These chapters promise life and beauty and abundance, and God Himself bookends it all.

He is Alpha and Omega. He is beginning and end.

DAY 39: THE END OF WAITING

He is the One who breathed anticipation into the world, and He is the One who will fulfill it.

That's why drawing near to God in the waiting spaces is so important. We meet God in the waiting. We get to know Him in our longing. We get to experience His love and grace here in the hard, middle places. And one day, when Jesus returns and we get to experience life in the fullness of God's presence—when we're no longer living in the shadow of what is—we'll recognize Him because we spent all that time building relationship with Him in the waiting.

Before we leave this space, let me leave you with this benediction:

Therefore, since we also have such a large cloud of witnesses surrounding us, let us lay aside every hindrance and the sin that so easily ensnares us. Let us run with endurance the race that lies before us, keeping our eyes on Jesus, the pioneer and perfecter of our faith. For the joy that lay before Him, He endured the cross, despising the shame, and sat down at the right hand of the throne of God. (Hebrews 12:1-2)

You're in good company in the waiting. Keep pressing on. Keep the lessons you've learned here close to your heart. Let them change you, and continue to draw near to God.

Ultimately, He is the One we're waiting for.

How have you felt the ache for God to set things right again?

In what ways does today's study encourage you in your own waiting?

Day 40: Your Name Here

After studying everyone else's stories, we're going to take some time to circle back to your own. I told you we would. Maybe on Day 1 you rolled your eyes at the thought of having to revisit your own waiting and got a little nervous, uncertain of how things would play out for you. Maybe you hoped that by the time you reached this page you'd have answers and have made at least some progress. Wherever you were when you began, it's time to reflect on where you've been and how far you've come. Take your time here. Allow this to be a space of honest reflection with God and to draw you closer to Him.

Why did you pick up this study?

Which person's story did you most resonate with and why?

Compare your relationship with God now to when you first started this study? Has anything changed?

Has there been any progress in your waiting? Even if circumstances aren't what you want, are there any ways you have seen growth or change?

How has God spoken to you through this study?

What's next for you? Is there another study you're going to pick up? Is God inviting you to lead someone else through this one? Have these last 40 days inspired a need to take a specific step?

Leader Resources

Welcome, leader! Bible study workbooks are a great way to help your group dig deep into Scripture. While *In the Waiting* is formatted as a daily study, you'll find a leader guide in the next few pages to guide you in leading a weekly meeting with this material.

This guide comes equipped with tips to help you lead well and weekly lessons to assist you in preparing for and facilitating 8 weekly meetings, with the option of extending into 10 weeks.

Each group session is outlined and includes a focus passage, discussion questions, prayer prompts, an ice breaker, and an optional worship song. Use as much or as little of this guide as you wish for your weekly meetings. This guide is merely here to help you get started.

Speaking of getting started, here are a few tips to keep in mind as you lead your group:

TIP #1 BE PREPARED

The mark of any good leader is the ability to direct people down a particular path or toward a specific goal. In the case of this study, our goal is to draw near to God and encounter Him in His Word, both as a group and individuals. But it's hard to lead where you haven't yet been. Don't skimp on your preparation time. While it may be tempting to rush to prepare your weekly meetings, you'll want to make sure you set aside enough time each week to prepare. That means working through the daily lessons yourself, and spending time in prayer for your group and your weekly meetings.

TIP #2 HAVE A RELATIONAL MINDSET

As you prepare and deliver lessons each week, don't forget that this study time is meant to be a relationship builder between you and God too. If you're going to lead your group well in drawing near to God in these waiting seasons, it's important that you are prioritizing your own relationship with God. That doesn't mean that you have to have it all together and be happy all the time. It does mean that you're being honest with God, yourself, and even your group about your relationship with the Lord and the season you're in. Don't just do the work of this study for the sake of leading others. Move through the study and these preparation materials as a way to build your own relationship with God.

TIP #3 GO FIRST

Waiting is a tough topic to dig into because it hits on very tender pieces of our hearts. Whether your group is new or you've met together for years, you as the leader will set the tone for the group in the areas of vulnerability and honesty. If those are things you want to cultivate in your group, you'll need to be prepared to go first in discussion, at least as you get started. Don't feel like you need to say everything or divulge your entire story, but vulnerability breeds vulnerability. If you're willing to be open and honest with your group, they will feel safe to open up and be vulnerable too.

TIP #4 CREATE A SAFE SPACE

Speaking of feeling safe, be sure to establish expectations and guidelines as your group gets going, so that everyone feels safe and has the appropriate space to share. Make sure everyone has an opportunity to share if they want to. Some people won't, and that's okay. Don't pressure anyone, but make sure you leave space and provide moments for people to share. Set a non-judgmental tone for the group. Let people know that what is shared in the group is safe and group members will be loved and supported. Work on building relationships with each group member individually. Try reaching out with a text message or phone call during the week. Pick a different person each week to intentionally have a one-on-one conversation with. When your group members feel invested in and valued by you they are more likely to feel safe in the group.

TIP #5 BE CONSISTENT AND ORGANIZED

Gathering a group together can be difficult. You will likely bump up against schedule conflicts and off-track conversations, in addition to other things. As your group starts meeting together, find a date and time that works for everyone for the duration of this study and stick with it. If a meeting needs to be rescheduled make sure there is a system in place to let your group know.

TIP #6 BE FLEXIBLE

While being organized and prepared is important, another mark of a good leader is flexibility. There may be weeks where one of your group members brings up something that throws your plans out the window. Be mindful of those. More than going through the material, your group time is about growing together and seeking God. Be mindful of what your group needs and be open to the Holy Spirit leading you in a different direction than what you planned.

TIP #7 BE IN PRAYER

The last tip I have for you is one you can begin implementing even before your group begins,

LEADER RESOURCES

and that is to be in prayer. Pray for your group members, for community to be developed. Pray for wisdom as you prepare to lead, and pray for relationships to flourish.

On the following pages you will find outlines for each week's lessons. Use these as a reference or guide to prepare for the meetings.

I pray that this time of meeting together in a community and working through this material is challenging, life-giving, and draws all of you closer to God.

Also, don't forget that you can access teaching videos that correspond with these weekly sessions at jazminnfrank.com/waiting.

LEADER RESOURCES

Optional Kick-off session

Theme: Getting Started

The purpose of this meeting is to get together to establish expectations and get to know each other a bit before you begin the study. If you are studying with a group that is already established, you can skip this session. Just make sure people read the Introduction and Bible Study Basics sections before your first meeting.

Even if you don't plan on having snacks at future meetings, sharing a meal or having snacks for this kick off session is a great idea!

Ice Breaker: 2 truths and a lie. Each person in the group takes a turn sharing three things about themselves--2 things are true, one is not. The rest of the group must figure out which one is the lie.

Read: As a group, read through the Introduction and Bible Study Basics sections of the study together. Tackle any questions or concerns your group has about this topic.

Plan: Fill out this group plan for when and where you will meet

Our group will meet from (start time)_____ to (end time)_____

We will meet on (day)_____

We will meet at (place)_____

We plan to meet from (date)_____ to (date)_____

Closing Prayer: Take time to pray for each group member by name as they embark on this study.

Assign Reading: Days 1-5

Week 1: Days 1-5

Theme: Beginning a Waiting Season

Objective: Waiting seasons can be difficult to manage. The goal for this week is to help your group members name their waiting and to recognize that waiting is not forever. It is only a season, but it's a season we can invite God into and get to know Him better as a result.

5 min **Ice Breaker:** Share about a time you waited for something and how that felt.

15 min **Weekly Catch Up:**

1. What stuck out to you from this week's reading?
2. Which person's story did you most connect with?
3. How did God speak to you this week?

2 min **Passage:** Ecclesiastes 3:1-8

15 min **Discussion:**

1. Are you in a waiting season? If so, what are you waiting for? (Some members may have already answered this in the ice breaker).
2. Share your thoughts about the idea of waiting as a season.
3. What comfort do you find in this week's passage, specifically when it comes to waiting seasons?
4. What kind of waiting season are you in? You may find it helpful to use words from today's passage.
5. How can we as a group support or encourage you in your own waiting?

(optional) Song: "Waiting Here for You" by Passion

20 min **Prayer and Connection Time:** Invite God into this season of study and this season of waiting.

Assign Reading: Days 6-10

LEADER RESOURCES

Week 2: Days 6-10

Theme: Remembering God's Presence

Objective: Seasons of waiting can sometimes cause us to feel like God is distant or that He is holding back from us. In this week's lesson, we're focusing on the truth that God is present with us in the waiting.

***5 min* Ice Breaker:** When was the last time you clearly experienced God's presence? Describe a time when you felt distant from God.

***15 min* Weekly Catch Up:**

1. What stuck out to you from this week's reading?
2. Which person's story did you most connect with?
3. How did God speak to you this week?

***2 min* Passage:** Lamentations 3:21-26

***15 min* Discussion:**

1. Do you feel close to God in your waiting or do you feel distant from Him?
2. What do you feel like you need from God right now?
3. What verses from today's passage give you comfort or encourage you in your waiting?
4. Verse 25 reminds us that the Lord is good to those who wait for Him. How do you see God's goodness in this season?

(optional) Song: "Give Me Faith" Elevation Worship

***20 min* Prayer and Connection Time:** Divide up today's passage and have everyone read a verse as a way to pray and praise communally. Take time to remember God's goodness and His ever-present presence in the waiting.

Assign Reading: Days 11-15

IN THE WAITING

Week 3: Days 11-15

Theme: Letting Waiting Shape You

Objective: As we wait, we are shaped. This can be a good or a bad thing. If we allow it to, our waiting seasons can cause us to become bitter and distant, but there is just as much opportunity to grow stronger, more mature, and more sure of God's goodness and faithfulness. This week we are wrestling with the idea that we get to choose how we let the waiting shape us.

5 min **Ice Breaker:** Share an experience from your life that shaped you into the person you are today.

15 min **Weekly Catch Up:**

1. What stuck out to you from this week's reading?
2. Which person's story did you most connect with?
3. How did God speak to you this week?

2 min **Passage:** Romans 4:18-5:5

15 min **Discussion:**

1. This passage is about Abraham and the covenant of faith God made with him. Abraham's wait was long and hard, but how was Abraham shaped through his wait?
2. Romans 5:3-5 talks about the progression of how suffering produces hope. Have you seen that progression lived out, either in your own life or in the life of another?
3. How might your perspective on waiting change if you inserted the word "waiting" in place of "suffering" in Romans 5:3-5?

(optional) Song: "Get Your Hopes Up" Josh Baldwin

20 min **Prayer and Connection Time:** Take time to confess your ideas and attitudes about waiting and ask God to use this season to shape you and produce hope.

Assign Reading: Days 16-20

LEADER RESOURCES

Week 4: Days 16-20

Theme: Finding Strength in the Waiting

Objective: When we think of waiting, many times it feels like a draining thing because waiting means we don't yet have that thing we want. Isaiah tells us, though, that waiting has a way of strengthening us. Waiting isn't a punishment. Its preparation. This week we are pressing into that truth, because once we see that, our whole interaction with God in the waiting changes.

5 min **Ice Breaker:** What do you do to rest up or restore your strength?

This is a great lead-in question to today's passage and exploring the idea that waiting can be something that strengthens us. Feel free to keep this in its normal position or save this question until after the weekly catch up time.

15 min **Weekly Catch Up:**

1. What stuck out to you from this week's reading?
2. Which person's story did you most connect with?
3. How did God speak to you this week?

2 min **Passage:** Isaiah 40:1-31

15 min **Discussion:**

1. This passage focuses a lot on God's character and nature. What do you learn about Him?
2. How does better understanding God's character help you in the waiting?
3. What image does Isaiah use to describe those that wait on the Lord? Why do you think he chose this image?
4. How do you see God strengthening you in the waiting?

(optional) Song: "Find You Here" Ellie Holcomb

20 min **Prayer and Connection Time:** Most of the time our desire is for God to end our waiting. Today, take some time to pray as a group or break up into smaller groups and praise God for the waiting and all the ways you are being strengthened in this season.

Assign Reading: Days 21-25

Week 5: Days 21-25

Theme: Persevering in the Waiting

Objective: Waiting requires time. It requires that we sit in that tension of wanting and not yet having, and that requires perseverance. In this week's lesson we'll explore what it looks like to persevere in the waiting even when you feel like giving up.

5 min **Ice Breaker:** Share one high and one low from your week.

15 min **Weekly Catch Up:**

1. What stuck out to you from this week's reading?
2. Which person's story did you most connect with?
3. How did God speak to you this week?

2 min **Passage:** Philippians 3:8-21, 4:4-9

15 min **Discussion:**

1. Has there been a moment in your waiting when you wanted to give up? What keeps you waiting a little longer?
2. In this passage, Paul is talking about persevering in the faith and how outward things don't matter as much as the inner faith journey. How does this passage guide or encourage you in the waiting?
3. Paul writes that all things are a loss compared to knowing Christ and that any suffering he faces is worth it. How do you feel about that in regards to that thing you're waiting for? If you never get it, but you get closer to God in the process, will it be enough?

(optional) Song: "Count Me In" by Switch

20 min **Prayer and Connection Time:** Give everyone time to share any personal requests then close out with a time of praise. Go around the group give everyone the opportunity to praise God for who He is.

Assign Reading: Days 26-30

LEADER RESOURCES

Week 6: Days 26-30

Theme: Have Courage

Objective: Waiting requires courage. It is a brave act to wait on God for something you haven't yet seen. It can be a hard and discouraging season. In this lesson, we'll explore the beauty of waiting with God and the courage to expect good things from Him.

5 min **Ice Breaker:** When have you experienced God's faithfulness in an abundant or beautiful way? How did that experience draw you closer to Him?

15 min **Weekly Catch Up:**

1. What stuck out to you from this week's reading?
2. Which person's story did you most connect with?
3. How did God speak to you this week?

2 min **Passage:** Psalm 27

15 min **Discussion:**

1. Have you had to face any enemies or discouragers in your season of waiting? People who thought your decision to wait wasn't worth it? How does that opposition make you feel?
2. David explores a beautiful kind of intimacy with God even in the midst of his struggles. How's your relationship with God? Are you continuing to grow in intimacy or are you holding Him at a distance?
3. Do you believe God is good? Do you believe God is good to you? Do you believe, like David in verse 13-14, that you will see God's goodness?
4. What does courage look like for you right now?

(optional) Song: "Fighting For Me" by Riley Clemmons

20 min **Prayer and Connection Time:** Take time to share any doubts the group is facing, bring them before God, and ask Him to increase belief and trust in God's goodness.

Assign Reading: Days 31-35

Week 7: Days 31-35

Theme: Waiting with Love

Objective: Often the waiting seasons can become very self-focused. We're focused on our pain or our lack. Those feelings and pain points aren't wrong, but waiting well also means looking up and loving those around you. Today we'll dig into a familiar passage about love and explore how it applies to our seasons of waiting.

5 min **Ice Breaker:** In what tangible or memorable ways have you received love from someone?

15 min **Weekly Catch Up:**

1. What stuck out to you from this week's reading?
2. Which person's story did you most connect with?
3. How did God speak to you this week?

2 min **Passage:** 1 Corinthians 13

15 min **Discussion:**

1. How does loving well help us wait well?
2. What aspect of love described in this passage do you feel you are doing well in and what area do you feel you need to grow in?
3. In what ways are you experiencing God's love in your waiting?

(optional) Song: "The Blessing" by Cody Carnes and Kari Jobe

20 min **Prayer and Connection Time:** Ask God to show you opportunities to love well this next week. Praise Him for the ways He has shown His love for you and ask Him to make you more aware of His love.

Assign Reading: Days 36-40

LEADER RESOURCES

Week 8: Days 36-40

Theme: Surrounded By Others Who Waited

Objective: Waiting has a way of isolating. We can feel left out because other people have what we are waiting for. Waiting can feel lonely, but we are not alone. Everyone has waited and is waiting for something. We've spent the last eight weeks studying people throughout Scripture who waited. Let's draw some encouragement from the fact that seasons of waiting are not nearly as isolating as they feel. In fact, waiting can be a connecting point with others.

5 min **Ice Breaker:** Who is your hero or someone you look up to when it comes to living devoted to God?

15 min **Weekly Catch Up:**

1. What stuck out to you from this week's reading?
2. Which person's story did you most connect with?
3. How did God speak to you this week?

2 min **Passage:** Hebrews 11:1-12:3

15 min **Discussion:**

1. The writer of Hebrews tells all of these stories of faith to encourage Christians to keep pressing toward the goal of knowing God. That has been the goal of our study together too. Of all the people in this passage and the stories we've studied together, whose story and faith has had the greatest impact on you and why? Whose story has been the most challenging and why?
2. How have you grown through this study? What's changed for you?
3. One of the beauties of a study like this is to be filled up so that you can go encourage someone else. How might you share what you've learned here with someone else?

(optional) Song: "You Never Let Go" by Bryan and Katie Torwalt

20 min **Prayer and Connection Time:** Approach God from a place of surrender. Ask Him for an opportunity to share what you've learned to encourage someone else in their waiting.

IN THE WAITING

Optional Celebration Session

Theme: Celebrate and Reflect

This session will be different from the others. Make plans ahead of time to come together around the table and enjoy some good food. Share a meal together and as you eat, give space for group members to share their responses to this final section of study.

Icebreaker: Gather together and get a picture of all of you to remember this season of seeking the Lord.

Discussion:

1. Use the reflection questions from Day 40 to share about what you've learned and how you've grown in this study.
2. Make plans for what is next for your group. Is there another study you would like to do together?

Closing prayer: Open the group in prayer and then leave space for group members to jump in with their own prayers. Pray for each other's needs. Pray prayers of worship and gratitude to God for how He moved through this study. Ask for His guidance about where to go and what to study next as a group, if your group plans to keep meeting.

Acknowledgements

The deeper I get into ministry, the more I'm convinced that this is a team effort, and the more I celebrate that fact. My team is one of the best. Behind every Bible study is a group of supportive, talented, truth-telling, Spirit-led people who make this possible, and it is my great pleasure turn the spotlight on them and highlight their pure awesomeness!

To my family: You've held me on the hard days, cheered me on, and celebrated with me as this ministry continues to grow. You've reminded to keep making writing a priority, and you have created space for me to that. You have supported me at every turn. I'm so grateful God gave me you.

To Taryn, my designer extraordinaire: Your knack for taking these words and packaging them beautifully for people is mind-blowing. How you manage to catch my vision with the few instructions I provide on color and design, I will never know. It's always a pleasure working with you. I'm so glad to have you on the Beautifully Devoted team!

To Anna-Stacia, my friend, fellow writer, and crafter of words: I'm grateful for your partnership, not only in this project, but in getting to do this writing-thing together. I know I always have a buddy to go to on those days when I freak out over a bad draft or when I need someone to convince me to keep seeking Jesus and keep writing the words He gives me even when it's hard. It's so fun celebrating milestones with you and sharing projects.

To my supporters—Brittany, Judy, Sara, Teresa, Patti, and Michele—the fact that you have invested in me, this work, and this ministry is so humbling. I'm not sure what you saw that made you think it was worth partnering up together, but I'm so glad you did.

To my mastermind group: Thank you for your endless encouragement, wisdom, insight, and support. You understand those aspects of the writing world that no one else does. You've provided so much encouragement this year as writing became my full-time job. I'm just happy to have you ladies as fellow sojourners on this writing journey.

To my bandmates, Ruthie and Stephanie: You have poured into me more than you can imagine. You are friends, but more than that, you are my sisters. You provided the space for me to work through these lessons of waiting in my own life before I ever put them to the page. Thank you for hearing me, letting me take up space in your homes, and for being so intentional in celebrating me and my work. I love doing life with you two and getting to grow together. You rock!

To my peer review bros, Jacob and Michael: Thank you, Michael, for letting me claim your couch as my office on days when I needed to work in a new space. Thank you, Jacob, for your many affirming words and hugs. I respect you both so much and value your opinions. You two are my top tier people when it comes to making sure I'm being true to Scripture and teaching in a way that is received by the dudes as well as the ladies. Thank you for taking the time to read early versions of this study and for your honest feedback. You guys made this study great!

To God: Words cannot express my gratitude that You have allowed me to do this work. Writing this study was hard, living it is even harder, but You have taught me so much about Your love and how You are present and gracious, no matter what season I am walking through. Nothing can separate me from You or Your love. In fact, even these hard waiting seasons are opportunities to know You more. Thank You for trusting me with these words and for blessing me with this team that has helped to make this project a reality.

And to you, dear reader: Thank you for trusting me to lead you down this road. I know it's a hard one, and I know I probably poked at some painful things, but I'm glad you stuck it out. Thank you for purchasing this book, for sharing it with a friend, for being brave and choosing to spend your time here. This has always been for you, and I hope that you've come out on the other end loving God, loving His story, and living devoted.

A Note from the Author

You did it! You made it to the end of this study, and I am so very proud of you for it. If this study impacted you in any way, I would love to hear from you. One of the greatest joys of this job is getting to hear people's stories of how God is working in their lives. If you have a story to share, I'd love to hear it! You can reach out to me on Instagram, Facebook, or send me an email. I'd love for us to stay connected!

jazmin.forhisglory@gmail.com
@jazminnfrank
Jazminnfrank.com

Don't forget to claim your bonuses!

Looking for more great content and resources to encourage you in your waiting season?

Visit jazminnfrank.com/waiting to claim your bonuses.

HERE'S WHAT YOU'LL FIND:

Music playlist
Downloadable resources
Audio devotional
Video teachings

Also Available

Learn more and download previews at jazminnfrank.com/books.

DEVOTED SCRIPTURE JOURNAL: A DAILY GUIDE TO LOVING GOD THROUGH HIS WORD

The *Devoted Scripture Journal* is a guided Bible study tool designed to restore the relational aspect of Bible study. In this accessible and adaptable journal, you'll find 13 weeks' worth of daily Bible study pages. These daily pages provide a simple, adaptable structure for Bible study with sections for prayer, writing the Word, digging deeper, claiming joy, and recording a truth to meditate on each day.

This journal also comes with other helpful resources to grow your relationship with God, including:

- weekly heart checks
- guided reflection for your season of life
- 30 day reading plan
- prayer pages
- 10 ways to revive your devotional routine

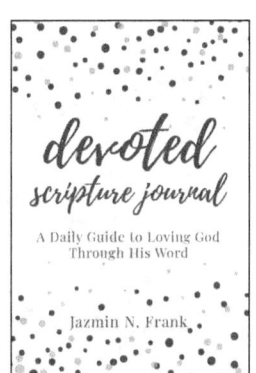

NAME ABOVE ALL NAMES: AN INVITATION TO REMEMBER WHO JESUS REALLY IS

This 31 day study through the gospel of John invites you to remember who Jesus is by focusing on the names of Jesus.

The names of Jesus tell us plainly who he is. They show us how we can relate to him, what he has accomplished, and in some cases, the names of Jesus also define us. So in remembering who Jesus is, we also are reminded of who we are in him.

Let this be the season you remember the name that is above every name—the name of Jesus. And in remembering him may you come to trust him more than you ever have before.

Do you have an idea for a Bible study? Looking for a study customized specifically for your group? Let's work together to make that happen!

Learn more at jazminnfrank.com/custom.

www.ingramcontent.com/pod-product-compliance
Lightning Source LLC
Chambersburg PA
CBHW051149290426
44108CB00019B/2658